JUNE JORDAN'S
POETRY FOR THE PEOPLE

JUNE JORDAN'S
POETRY FOR THE PEOPLE

A Revolutionary Blueprint

edited by Lauren Muller
and
the Poetry for the People Collective

Shanti Bright
Gary Chandler
Ananda Esteva
Sean Lewis
Stephanie Rose
Shelly Smith
Shelly Teves
Rubén Antonio Villalobos
Pamela Wilson

Routledge ! New York & London

Published in 1995 by
Routledge
29 West 35th Street
New York, NY 10001

Published in Great Britain by
Routledge
11 New Fetter Lane
London EC4P 4EE

The excerpt from "Blood, Bread, and Poetry: The Location of the Poet" is reprinted from *Blood, Bread and Poetry: Selected Prose 1979–1985* by Adrienne Rich, by permission of the author and W.W. Norton and Company, Inc. © 1986 by Adrienne Rich. "Travelin' Shoes (for June Jordan)" by Ruth Forman was originally published in *Women's Studies Quarterly*, Summer 1994, Vol. XXII, nos. 1 & 2, pp. 51–53. Permission to reprint granted by the author. "Poetry Should Ride the Bus" and "For Your Information" by Ruth Forman were originally published in *We Are the Young Magicians*, © 1993 by Ruth Forman, reprinted by permission of Beacon Press. The lines from "Power" are reprinted from *The Black Unicorn: Poems* by Audre Lorde, by permission of W.W. Norton and Company, Inc. © 1978 by Audre Lorde. The excerpt from Joy Harjo's "Writing with the Sun" was originally published in *Where We Stand: Women Poets on Literary Tradition*, ed. Sharon Bryan (New York: W.W. Norton and Company, Inc. © 1993), pp. 70–74, and is reprinted by permission of the poet. June Jordan's poems "Something Like A Sonnet for Phillis Miracle Wheatly" and "Free Flight," and short quotations from *Voice of the Children* and *Soulscript: Afro-American Poetry* are all reprinted courtesy of the author.

Library of Congress Cataloging-in-Publication Data

June Jordan's Poetry for the People: a revolutionary blueprint / edited by Lauren Muller and the Poetry for the People Collective; with an introduction by June Jordan.

   p. cm.
   ISBN 0-415-91167-2 (cloth) — ISBN 0-415-91168-0 (paper)

   1. Poetry for the People (Organization) 2. American poetry—20th century—History and criticism—Theory, etc. 3. Americn poetry—Study and teaching (Higher)—California—Berkeley. 4. American poetry—minority authors—History and criticism—Theory, etc. 5. Poetry—Societies, etc.—History—20th century. 6. Poetry—Authorship. 7. Jordan, June, 1936– . I. Muller, Lauren. II. Jordan, June, 1936– . III. Poetry for the People (Organization)

PS301.J86 1995
808.1'007—dc20

95-8470
CIP

CONTENTS

Part Two
TAKING POETRY BACK TO THE PEOPLE

ACKNOWLEDGMENTS

We thank our literary agent, Frances Goldin, for her wonderful commitment to our project and her determination to get this Blueprint out into the world.

Thank you to Jayne Fargnoli, our extraordinary editor at Routledge, for her dedication to the values and highest ambitions underlying this entire project. Thank you also to Adam Bohannon, editorial and production manager, for his vision, patience, and hard work.

We give heartfelt thanks to the following writers, artists, and editors, without whom this book could not have been created: Alegria Barclay, Lisa von Blanckensee, Hal BrightCloud, Carla Helen-Toth, Jennifer Lim, Paul Manly, Nina Markov, Claudia May, Elizabeth Meyer, Maiana Minahal, Seth Moglen, Kelly Navies, Thomas O'Brien, Christine Renner, Carolyn Rice, Elena Serrano, Jacqueline Shea Murphy, Leslie Shown, Pamela Stafford, Albert Tong, Marianne Villalobos (Rubén's mom), Dorothy Wang, and Jing Zhang. Special thanks and love to Elmirie Robinson, who provided constant support.

Special thanks, also, to Poetry for the People guest poets and friends who responded to our questions on the canon and/or provided us with reading lists for our In-Your-Face-America bibliographies: Alfred Arteaga, Dan Bellm, Marilyn Chin, VèVè Clark, Cornelius Eady, Janice Gould, Joy Harjo, Ella Mae Lentz, David Lloyd, Jennifer Nelson, Leroy Quintana, and Ntozake

Shange. We also acknowledge other esteemed guests who gave readings and/or lectures for Poetry for the People: Charles Altieri, Thulani Davis, Yusef Komunyakaa, Li-Young Lee, Donna Masini, Erskine Peters, Jimmy Santiago Baca, Susan Schweik, Peter Dale Scott, and Sherley Anne Williams. Many, many thanks to Adrienne Rich for her generosity, encouragement, and inspiration.

We also acknowledge the good work of Leslie Simon, who founded an entirely different program called Poetry for the People at San Francisco City College. It was active from 1955 to 1984. Proclaiming that poetry for the people is "a modern day incarnation of a very old practice," the poets read and distributed their work publicly, from city parks to the county jail.

For constant and continued support, we sincerely thank the following members of the University of California at Berkeley administration, faculty, and staff: Chancellor Chang-Lin Tien; Vice Chancellor and Provost Carol Christ; Dean of Undergaduate and Interdisciplinary Studies Donald McQuade; Professor Margarita Melville; Dean Gerald Mendelsohn; Dr. Alix Schwartz; the departments of Asian American Studies, Chicana/o Studies, English, Ethnic Studies, and Women's Studies; Eric Anderson at the Alumni House; Chris Murchison and the staff at Foothill Residential Hall.

Thank you to Donald Palmer and Leila May, Lauren's patient downstairs neighbors who endured our noisy late-night writing sessions.

Our special thanks for the angelic support from the African American Studies Department, the office of the Vice Chancellor of Undergraduate Affairs, and the Ford Foundation—particularly to African American Studies Chair Percy Hintzen and former Chair Margaret Wilkerson; the African American Studies staff: Frances Carter, Johnnie Dilliehunt, Stephanie Jackson, and Marguerite Versher; Vice Chancellor of Undergraduate Affairs Genaro Padilla and former Vice Chancellor of Undergraduate Affairs W. Russell Ellis.

Of course, we thank all the poets and student teacher poets who have contributed their hearts and souls to Poetry for the People, especially those who regularly perform essential behind-the-scenes work, and whose commitment and enthusiasm make the collective enterprise possible.

And finally, we thank June Jordan for her brilliance and deep love for poetry and Poetry for the People.

— The Poetry for the People Blueprint Collective, U.C. Berkeley 1995

INTRODUCTION

June Jordan

June rallying with
her students.
(photo by Stephanie Rose)

PART ONE

Standing room only audience response, de facto coalition, widely coveted anthology publication, and written down empowerment through language: These are a few of the ways the world has welcomed Poetry for the People and the students this program seeks to serve. Our success at U.C. Berkeley has been so multifaceted and cumulative that, today, four and a half years after its inception, the program of Poetry for the People enjoys full academic accreditation and a huge population of young Americans who want to read and write poetry.

In this manual, readers will find out how to do it.

How to make sure that every single wannabe poet becomes a distinctive voice that people will listen to

How to assure the creation of a community of trust despite serious and sometimes conflictual baseline components of diversity: race, language, sexuality, class, age and gender

How to set things up so that student poets become teacher poets

How to develop a syllabus that reflects and respects the cultural heterogeneity of in-your-face America

How to rescue the "Canon" from well-deserved disrepute and make it relevant again

How to raise the money

How to get on the radio or work yourself into the local newspapers

How to put together a classroom anthology and a literary context so that young Americans can become familiar with the function and varieties of poetry coming from places as diverse as Ireland and South Central L.A.

Finally, **how to** be Super-Politically-Correct and therefore **how to** pursue a defensible mode of creative education as we approach the 21st century.

PART TWO

This is an important, big book of good news. While professional theoreticians and politicians debate "student participation" and while cheap-shot opinion-makers bemoan the "balkanization" of America or the "decline" of "Western civilization," something actual and positive and tested and new and very American has been happening here where I teach. While very well-paid and unqualified, non-geneticists have splashed their invidious notions of genetic destiny all over collaborating mass-media screens and printed pages, something else, something faithful and literate and individual and collective and technical and creative and systematic and unexpected and unpredictable has been taking place on the showcase campus of U. C. Berkeley.

Revered as a world-class university for scientific research and accomplishment, respected as the leading public institution of higher learning in the United States, and boasting the most heterogeneous student population on earth, the intellectual facts about U. C. Berkeley altogether disprove and debunk those popular armchair jitters variously headlined as "The Threat of Diversity" or "Political-Correctness-versus-Everything-Profound-and-Obviously-Indispensable-and-Unarguably-Critical-to-Enlightenment"— such as "Sir Gawain and the Green Knight."

But what's new inside the national example of U. C. Berkeley is not Chemistry or Nuclear Micro-Biology or Ultra-English Lit or Engineering or Women's Studies. It is not Pulitzer Prizes and MacArthur Foundation Awards regularly collected by illustrious members of the faculty. Nor is it the non-white majority freshmen culled from the very top of graduating high school seniors nationwide. The news is poetry.

And this important, big book documents the meaning of impassioned embrace of language, the meaning of that highest calling: the difficult, fabulous pursuit of the power of the word/the voice/the poetry, of people who live and die together, mostly unknown to each other: mostly seen, but not heard.

You cannot write lies and write good poetry. Deceit, abstraction, euphemism: any one of these will doom a poem to the realm of "baffling" or "forgettable," or worse. Good poetry requires precision: if you do not attempt to say, accurately, truthfully, what you feel or see or need, then how will you achieve precision? What criterion will guide you to the next absolutely "right" word?

And so poetry is not a shopping list, a casual disquisition on the colors of the sky, a soporific daydream, or bumpersticker sloganeering. Poetry is a political action undertaken for the sake of information, the faith, the exorcism, and the lyrical invention, that telling the truth makes possible. Poetry means taking control of the language of your life. Good poems can interdict a suicide, rescue a love affair, and build a revolution in which speaking and listening to somebody becomes the first and last purpose to every social encounter.

I would hope that folks throughout the U.S.A. would consider the creation of poems as a foundation for true community: a fearless democratic society.

This important, big book delivers a blueprint for poetry for the people: a testament, a manual, an anthology of new poems and new bibliographies, and an open case history. It is an academic experiment soaring past campus boundaries. It is a political movement that anybody anywhere can join, imitate, or improve. It is a literary movement that no one can stifle or erase.

But I did not wake up one morning ablaze with a coherent vision of Poetry for the People! The natural intermingling of my ideas and my observations as an educator, a poet, and the African-American daughter of poorly documented immigrants did not lead me to any limiting ideological perspectives or resolve. Poetry for the People is the arduous and happy outcome of practical, day-by-day, classroom failure and success.

For anyone interested, this Blueprint will spare you most of the trial and many of the errors of my own gradual discoveries.

All of my teaching life I have tried to remember how much I always, as a student, hated school, and why. It is, in some ways, quite amazing for me to realize that, as of this date, I have been a teacher, on the University level, for almost two decades. Now it would seem very strange, and I would feel grievously deprived, if I did not need to think in new ways and read many new books and learn new names and adapt to a new and unpredictable racial and cultural heterogeneity of specific breadth in experience, every semester.

When I was going to school, too much of the time I found myself an alien body force-fed stories and facts about people entirely unrelated to me, or my family. And the regular demands upon me only required my acquiescence to a program of instruction predetermined without regard for my particular history, or future. I was made to learn about "the powerful": those who won wars or who conquered territory or whose odd ideas about poetry and love prevailed inside some distant country where neither my parents nor myself would find welcome.

When I arrived at the University of California at Berkeley, the outdoor student society of competing opinions and conflicting/comingling identities inflamed my imagination. I wondered if I could try to preserve, and even embolden, that fabulous, natural energy of assertive, polemical young hearts and minds inside the classroom.

My first semester teaching for African American Studies and Women's Studies Departments tested these ambitions, at once. When I walked into the classroom for African American Freshman Composition, to my complete surprise, I found a minority of African American students: the majority presented me with an uneasy mix of Asian American and Chicana/Chicano Americans and Euro-Americans. My task, then, was to revise and to devise a reading list and a method of handling diverse writings so as to identify, and embrace, what was distinctive to African American experience, on the one hand, and also, to identify, and to embrace, what was personally relevant (either because of commonalities or because of important differences) to every young man and woman sitting in that same space.

When I walked into my first Women's Studies classroom, I found myself facing an overwhelmingly White group of young women packed together in an expectant, rabble-rousing spirit that completely surprised me: What were they expecting? What did they want to happen?

In African American Studies Freshman Composition, I quickly developed a practical value system which invested student writing with at least as much imperative worth as anything else we might read. This meant student compositions twice weekly, at least, and this meant that, in effect, the class was producing its own literature: a literature reflecting the ideas and dreams and memories of the actual young Americans at work.

For the Women's Studies, I quickly settled upon the concept of "The Politics of Childhood" and, to my delight, the students eagerly rallied to that challenge. In addition to our assigned readings, they wrote and they shared, aloud, whatever had deeply bruised, or enabled, them as children. Before long, we had reason to declare our class "A Community of Trust." The honesty and the depth of students' sharing required no less, if we were to proceed as a collective. Eventually, the pain of so much of the testimony became perilously keen and threatened to immobilize/demoralize all participants. At this point, I tried to invent a route to power: I asked students to conduct research into the status of children in California, and in other parts of the U.S.A. I asked them to organize their findings and then integrate their individual lives, as children, into the big picture of children's needs unmet, in our America. This they did with fantastic, evangelical energy and competence, both.

I contacted KPFA, and was able to arrange for an hour-long broadcast of student-researched/student-composed/student-performed script. So successful was this event that KPFA re-broadcast this offering and Pacifica National Radio put the show on nationwide satellite. In addition, calls and letters to the students came pouring in from people working with abused children: child advocates, moved by the power of the students' knowledge and purposes. And, at the end, a new organization advocating children's rights was formed, with University of California at Berkeley students of the class, "The Politics of Childhood" at its helm.

As a teacher I was learning how not to hate school: how to overcome the fixed, predetermined, graveyard nature of so much of formal education: come and be buried here among these other (allegedly) honorable dead.

For my next semester, I undertook the presentation of Contemporary Women's Poetry and African American Poetry. Again, student writings occupied equal space and time, along with James Weldon Johnson or

Adrienne Rich, for example. But, still, there seemed to be something inherently backwards and/or inert to our studies. At last, I realized it would be logical, and terrific, to publish the students' poetry in their own anthologies. We would distribute these books at public student readings organized and publicized with at least as much care and determination as we might give to a campus appearance by a visiting Hot Shot Poet.

And so, "Poetry November" was born. In this month, African American Poetry students and Contemporary Women's Poetry students would, separately, present their poems on campus. Their anthologies would be given to the audience. And their readings would receive press and radio and flyer publicity altogether commensurate to the publicity we would muster for the two visiting poets, Cornelius Eady and Sherley Anne Williams, we intended to invite.

To make all of this happen, I raised money: from the African American Studies Department to the Dean of Interdisciplinary Studies to the Department of English. And the students raised money from various student funding sources. Suddenly a huge beehive of multifaceted activity exploded into life: Poetry November was on its way!

We were listed with the *San Francisco Chronicle* Pink Pages, *Poetry Flash*, *The Daily Californian*, and the students and myself went on the air on KPFA and KQED, and, it seemed, things would come together.

Then we decided to have a reception of food and beverages and flowers after each reading. African American Poetry students would buy the food and set-up the reception and host everything for the Contemporary Women's Poetry reading. And vice-versa. As a result of this exchange plan, students met in myriad committee and errand gang activities and became allies and friends across pretty important former barriers. For example, I remember my happy shock when I saw a young White lesbian student and a young Black student, a nationalist young man, laughing and dancing around with a vacuum cleaner in the cleanup aftermath of a reception held in the English Department's lounge.

Each student reading was Standing Room Only. Ditto for the Hot Shot Poet's evening. In response to this response, and in recognition of the willingness of truly disparate students to work together, closely, when the factor of self-interest is clear (the common goal of a successful public poetry reading) I decided to try and vault beyond the demarcations of Women's Studies and African American Studies and, instead, offer something called "Poetry for the People."

This dream-reality began with my third semester at U.C. Berkeley. Students from Freshmen to graduate students in their last year at Boalt Law

School, men/women, African Americans, Asian Americans, Latino Americans, Euro Americans, gay, lesbian, straight—everybody, The People—could take this course in poetry. Requirements stipulated common readings and discussion, obedience to a tyrannical set of guidelines that I composed, a hefty minimum number of acceptable poems to be written by each student, energetic help with publishing the anthology, raising monies for this objective, and participation in a public poetry reading that would include all of the tedious tasks attendant to publicity and a small reception, afterwards.

These requirements were met by the enthusiastic throng of students who came to Poetry for the People. As the Gulf War was then in progress, the students' anthology was called "Poetry for the People in A Time Of War." Various students gave interviews to the Bay Area Press and, again, appeared on KPFA and KQED, and so forth.

Towards the end of the previous semester I had conceived, organized, and directed a campus-wide "Teach-in" on the Persian Gulf War. Faculty colleagues of many disciplines, and student activists of several ideologies, and of every color and ethnicity and sexual persuasion fused their energies to create a very powerful day that was decently documented by local television, radio and press. Ours was, I might add, proudly, the first such "Teach-in" in the U.S.A.

The huge success of "Poetry November" and the Gulf War "Teach-in" transformed my expectations. Evidently, at last, I had become part of an academic community where you could love school because school did not have to be something apart from, or in denial of, your own life and the multifarious new lives of your heterogeneous students! School could become, in fact, a place where students learned about the world and then resolved, collectively and creatively, to change it!

At the conclusion of the third semester, a core of young poets wanted to make Poetry for the People a way of life. And we discussed what to do next. I decided to try and institute a course called "The Teaching and Writing of Poetry." Interested students would work closely with me and then they, in turn, would become student teachers of other students. This was something we implemented with reasonable success.

Publication of the students' work, plus presentation of the students in a public reading, of course, continued to be fundamental attributes of both the Teaching and Writing of Poetry course and (its related) Poetry for the People. Again, the diversity of my students compelled a diversity of syllabus materials that I began to find mind-boggling. And, again, students collaborated together and became friends across every possible, previous barrier of distinction. I was pretty happy!

We, Poetry for the People, brought Adrienne Rich and Thulani Davis to the University of California at Berkeley, and later, Ntozake Shange, as well. We filled Wheeler Auditorium and, again, student readings were, themselves, S.R.O.

And with the sturdy expansion of our program, it did/does seem that there really are ways to change school so that you can get out of it more alive than dead!

If you value what students can teach to each other and to you,

If you spend at least half of your energies trying to connect students with the world on important, risky, levels of exchange and collaboration,

If you delete taglines like "multi-cultural" or "gender" or "sexual preference" from your brain and, instead, look to see who are the students you hope to interest, inform, include, and enlighten—through the literature you assign as well as through the sharing of the new American writings you will invite and enable them to create,

If you dream and scheme about the self-evident, as well as the potential, reasons why public performance, publication, and media appearances are natural and necessary steps to the acquirement of power through language,

Then: You will probably find yourself launched on an unpredictable, nerve-racking, and marvelous adventure in democracy and education!

But! Why should power and language coalesce in poetry? Because poetry is the medium for telling the truth, and because a poem is antithetical to lies/evasions and superficiality, anyone who becomes a practicing poet has an excellent chance of becoming somebody real, somebody known, self-defined, and attuned to and listening and hungering for kindred real voices utterly/articulately different from his or her own voice.

This outward and inward attunement seems to me a most reasonable basis for the political beginning of a beloved community: a democratic state in which the people can trust the names they have invented for themselves and for each other. It is this trustworthy use of words that poetry requires, and inspires. It is this highest ideal of trustworthy intersection among differing peoples that poetry can realize: POETRY FOR THE PEOPLE!

P.S. Several of the Poets for the People have become teachers themselves, and have presented their poetry to local high school student audiences, and so forth. In addition, other Poets for the People, including Pamela Wilson, Gary Chandler, Stephanie Rose, Dineale DeGidio, and Lisa von Blanckensee have formed a collective task force which works with elementary school children in the Bay Area on a regular basis.

Poetry for the People alumna Shelly Smith has established a poetry workshop in San Francisco: she turns no one away!

In his junior year at U.C. Berkeley, Poet for the People Michael Datcher conceived the idea of a national anthology of Black men's poetry. In his senior year, in fact, Michael Datcher followed through with extreme success and published the outstanding collection, *My Brother's Keeper*. He now leads a poetry workshop in Los Angeles, where he lives, and studies at U.C.L.A.

In her senior year at U.C. Berkeley, Poet for the People Ruth Forman submitted a manuscript of her poetry in the Barnard New Women Poet's Prize Competition and she won! In the following year, 1993, Beacon Press published Ruth Forman's *We Are the Young Magicians* which has met with the happiest possible critical acclaim, nationwide.

In 1994, Poet for the People Samiya Bashir was named Poet Laureate of the nine campuses of the University of California. Gary Chandler, Doris Lopez, and Claudia May received honorable mention in the U.C. Berkeley Chancellor's Prize for Poetry.

As a consequence of the Lila Wallace-Reader's Digest Award, which I have received for 1995–1998, I am collaborating with the eminent Japanese American poet, Janice Mirikitani, and several of my students in the establishment of a Poetry for the People at Glide Memorial Church in San Francisco!

And so on and on!

All of these victories bespeak a powerful fresh outreach to the environment surrounding the poet. There are other, more typical kinds of victories that mean that the poet is able to tell his father that he needs his father's love and the poet is able to name, and therefore exorcise the demons of incest abuse, and the poet is able to validate the duality he or she inherits as the child of a "mixed" marriage, and the poet is able to insist upon his or her own language—be it Korean/Spanish/Black English/or late 20th-Century straight-up lyrical Rap!

And within the tenuous experiment of a poetry workshop: of a beloved community, these young American men and women devise their individual trajectories into non-violent, but verifiable, power.

I think this is Sam from Gaia— talk to her about how to get involved.

Part One

TEACHING AND WRITING A NOW! BREED OF POETRY

June Jordan and
Elmirie Robinson

Cornelius Eady, guest poet,
and Percy Hintzen, Chair of
the African-American Studies
Department at U.C. Berkeley

June and students and
alumnae of Poetry for the
People

Ntombi Hollow,
poet and facilitator,
Glide Memorial Church

Maiana Minahal

(All photos courtesy of June Jordan)

1

PERSONAL AND POLITICAL POWER IN POETRY

POETRY FOR THE PEOPLE: A COURSE DESCRIPTION

June Jordan's Poetry for the People class of sixty to seventy students meets
once a week for three hours. Our class session typically begins with a twenty
minute "open mike" period in which students try out new poems. Then June,
a guest speaker or several student teacher poets will lecture on a particular
poetic genre, history, or tradition. Corresponding to assigned readings, the
lectures provide a foundation for in-depth study of different traditions of
American poetry, including African American, Asian American, Chicano/a
, Irish, Native American, women's poetry and "White" poetry—poetry
written by White men established inside "the canon." After discussing the
lecture, we take a short break, then subdivide into smaller workshop groups
to critique weekly poetry writing assignments. Facilitated by two to three
student teacher poets, these groups of five to ten "new" poets work together
during the entire semester. (Students may apply to become student teacher
poets after taking the Poetry for the People course at least once and working
closely with June in a seminar on teaching and writing poetry.) Outside class,
we meet in committees to organize public readings, assemble an anthology of
our own poetry, and create programs to take Poetry for the People into our
neighborhoods. In addition, the student teacher poets meet with June and

her graduate student teaching assistant once a week for two hours to critique their own poetry and to discuss teaching strategies, problems, and successes. Both June and the student teachers hold office hours every week.

On the first day of class, June introduces the organizing theme for the semester, such as "Whose Country Is This Anyway?" (Spring 1995) or "Poetry for the People In A Season of Love" (Spring 1994). The student teacher poets inaugurate the "open mike" tradition by reading or reciting their own poetry. Then June hands out the Poetry for the People course description and ground rules, as well as her "Guidelines for Writing and Critiquing A Poem" (Chapter 2) and a syllabus (Chapter 5).

The poets of Poetry
for the People.
Spring 1995.
(photo by
Abraham Lee)

Poetry for the People: A Course Description

1. We reach towards the development of literacy in today's world literature of poetry.

2. We divide our course of study, evenly, between the scrutiny of published poems, and the development of a new American poetry to be written by the students themselves.

3. We present this new American poetry in public readings open to the entire San Francisco Bay Area. These readings are invariable factors of coursework.

4. We publish student poetry in suitably splendid form, and distribute these anthologies at the student readings and through the kind offices of Berkeley bookstores, such as Black Oak Books and Cody's. This is an integral part of coursework.

5. In conjunction with coursework, we invite one or more visiting poets to present their work. These presentations are advertised throughout the San Francisco Bay Area, take place on campus, and are freely available to everyone. To date, we have presented Jimmy Santiago Baca, Marilyn Chin, Cornelius Eady, Thulani Davis, Joy Harjo, Li-Young Lee, Donna Masini, Adrienne Rich, Ntozake Shange, and Sherley Ann Williams. Obviously, our guiding criterion, in addition to that of excellence in poetry, is the relentless pursuit of ethnic, racial, gender, and linguistic diversity.

6. True to the concept of this program, all students, regardless of academic discipline or status (Freshmen to Graduate) are eligible for enrollment.

Ground Rules for Poetry for the People

Poetry for the People started as a program for political and artistic empowerment of students at U.C. Berkeley. Originating inside a public institution, and enjoying full academic accreditation, there are certain ground rules that must be respected inside this experimental, and hopeful, society:

1. "The People" shall not be defined as a group excluding or derogating anyone on the basis of race, ethnicity, language, sexual preference, class, or age.

2. "The People" shall consciously undertake to respect and to encourage each other to feel safe enough to attempt the building of a community of trust in which all may try to be truthful and deeply serious in the messages they craft for the world to contemplate.

3. Poetry for the People rests upon a belief that the art of telling the truth is a necessary and a healthy way to create powerful, and positive, connections among people who, otherwise, remain (unknown and unaware) strangers. The goal is not to kill connections but, rather, to create and to deepen them among truly different men and women.

CLAIMING AND PROCLAIMING OUR VOICES

Although Poetry for the People works within an academic structure, we push against its confines. Our attempt to integrate publishing and public presentations and guest lectures and small workshop groups (all at once) creates a constant, reeling momentum. What makes it all come together, come alive, is the centrality of our own voices.

Poetry names what has been silenced and allows us to understand and articulate our connections to one another and to the world we inhabit. In the spirit of the open microphone, we offer the following testimonies to the exuberance, necessity and audacity of Poetry for the People. We hope to provoke you to write, read and teach more poetry.

Poet Sean Lewis at the
open mike.
(photo by June Jordan)

Poetry as Revelation

Rubén Antonio Villalobos

In *Blood, Bread, and Poetry*, Adrienne Rich describes poetry as "revelation, information, a kind of teaching" (See Chapter 4). I absolutely agree. But when I was a child, this couldn't have been further from the truth. A mixture of Panamanian, White, and Jewish, I found no cultural role models in the people I was told about in school, least of all the poets of the canon.

We spent roughly two weeks a year on poetry, focusing on a few writers presented in the brief poetry chapter in our textbook, "Masterpieces of Western Literature," or something of that nature. In the fifth grade, my teacher spent these two weeks trying to teach us meter. "This poetry is said: da-daa, da-daa, da-daa, da-daa.... Repeat after me." She soon gave up, proclaiming that we had no rhythm. Imagine that! We could moonwalk from the classroom to the lunch line, but we "had no rhythm." Needless to say, I saw no revelation. In seventh grade, we were expected to imitate forms that we knew nothing about. Like all of my friends, I went to the library and found a book of haikus; they were short and easy. I copied a few down, word for word, and got an "A" on the project. But I did not feel informed. Throughout high school, poetry was presented like a game of Trivial Pursuit. I could recite "The New Colossus," memorize "great" poets' birthdays for an exam, and could even give an educated guess as to what Coleridge was smoking when he wrote "Kubla Khan," yet I hardly felt that I had received any of Adrienne Rich's "kind of teaching." Nothing that I learned or heard touched my heart. My teachers failed to present me with a method to approach poetry, and therefore kept me out of the Poetry Clubhouse, which was reserved only for the privileged few.

My senior year English teacher gave me a boost to the hard-to-reach first limb of the Poetry Club treehouse. Mr. Autry (a.k.a. "Yoda," who also happened to be my fencing coach, and was therefore beyond cool) read poetry aloud before us, and asked us to do the same. He explained Shakespeare's sonnets, sans "wherefore's" and "thou's." In "My mistress' eyes are nothing like the sun," Shakespeare disses his friends and bags on his mistress, while extolling her virtues at the same time! Now that, we could understand! By the end of the semester, we wrote sonnets and actually made money selling them at a Valentine's Day fundraiser for the Holden Caulfield Memorial Fencing Society. Dressed in full fencing regalia, we got on our knees and read sonnets to our clients' sweethearts, for only two dollars! Touché! I began to feel like a writer. No longer a poetry virgin, I read Herrick, and felt confident enough to imitate his repetition of sounds. Yet something was missing. While I could appreciate the works of the canon, I found little to relate to my own poetry, and my mixed cultural identity.

In my first Poetry for the People class, I began reading (and sometimes meeting) poets I had never heard of, poets who were writing in their own voices and in their own languages about real life issues that made sense. I saw how June Jordan uses line breaks to add meaning to each word, how Marylin Chin uses food to tie her words into a cultural knapsack, how Otto Rene Castillo uses the simplest language possible to indict his country's ruling class, and how Gloria Anzaldúa claims and proclaims her myriad identities. Each poet gave me a new tool, and I wanted to use what I learned from them to release stories from my own twenty-one years of experience.

Last year, I used my developing skills as a poet to tell my story in a letter to my Tío Juancho, who lives in Panamá and is like a grandfather to me. The poem begins with a child's queries about the things in Panamá that amazed me: sleeping grass, milk plants, the banana tree, the coconut candy my uncle makes every day to support his family. And mi tío answers my questions by mixing stories and songs, sweetened with just enough sugarcane honey to balance the bitter lessons of living in an occupied state. With the warm balls of cocada that he gives me, this wise man with no formal education sings to me the art, political science, and economics of our homeland.

As the poem continues, it reflects my coming of age as a Panamanian American, existing on the fifth border, living between two cultures. Unlike most countries with northern, eastern, southern, and western borders, Panamá also has a bisecting fifth border, the Panamá Canal Zone. This influence undermines the sovereignty of Panamá, a creature whose only predator, the United States, claims to protect it. In the excerpt below, I seek connections between the songs mi tío sang and current political events in Panamá.

Last summer, my mother translated "Tío Juancho" into Spanish while traveling home to Panamá. Upon arriving in our village, Monagrillo, she read the poem to family members who had gathered to welcome her. Tío Juancho was proud to hear a poem written about him, but the poem had greater impact on another uncle who was visiting Panamá after having been away for fifteen years. He started crying, and he told my mother that my poem awakened long-buried feelings for his family and country. In Monagrillo, my words returned a gift to my uncle—the same uncle who, fifteen years earlier, had taught me how to ride a bike in Modesto, California. As a new poet, I am not just on the receiving end of knowledge: I am now connected to my motherland through a biflowing cord of revelation, information, and teaching.

from *Tío Juancho*   Rubén Antonio Villalobos

sing to me, tío
take me to our land
take me to my land
show me how to work
the ground abuelo worked
how to feel the dirt
under my fingernails
show me the hut he built
where abuelita bore nine children
show me the land she loved
the land she left
the man she left
to educate her daughters
to give them a chance
'cause in the fields
they had none.

sing to me, tío
sing me the songs that tell me why
the dormideros
the milk plants
the blossoming bananas
and mis sueños Panameños
do not grow in this infertile land
take me by the hand
as you did so many years ago…

take mi tío
show me every plant, every mountain
every bird, every life-giving stream
but also show me
the dirty dollar, the endless squalor
bitter fruits of a broken pan-american dream

sing to me, tío
teach me the songs of the birds
i've never seen fly
teach me
the songs i do not
remember
or maybe,
the songs i never knew

Rubén Antonio Villalobos
captivates a crowd at a
Poetry for the People
reading.
(photo by June Jordan)

Rubén Antonio Villalobos *recently graduated from the University of California, Berkeley, with a degree in Ethnic Studies. Born in Modesto, California, he grew up in the United States and South America. He plans on doing as much as he can over the next few years, before he gets old at twenty-five.*

A Poet is on The Front Lines

Kelly Elaine Navies

I wrote my first poem, entitled "What is Life?,"at the age of eight. Basically, I copied the structure of another poem, "What is Love?," by a locally famous poet, Robert Woods. From then on, I kept a journal and wrote poems that were either too abstract to be meaningful to anyone other than myself, or were generic pieces acknowledging Black beauty, Black pride, and Black oppression, issues that spoke to my growing understanding of myself as an African American woman.

I began to discover the political significance of my own voice in Poetry for the People, in a classroom filled with stories: stories of political oppression, sexual rape, the psychological rape of miseducation, domestic violence and loss of language, stories of love stomped on and love celebrated. In the midst of all this intensity, abundant laughter still filled the room. June showered us with serious words of profundity: "Tell it. Tell us. Choose your words carefully. Say it simply, but be precise. Move me. We got work to do."

In this cauldron of tales, I begin to write about the abortion I had at age seventeen, an experience that taught me the issue of abortion is much more complex than the public debate between pro-choice and so-called pro-life. It's about me at seventeen on the way to U.C.L.A., pregnant and too ashamed, too independent, too stupid, too proud to ask anyone for help or advice—even the father of the unborn child. It's about hearing my father say over and over, "Abortion is murder. If you ever get pregnant give the baby to me." It's about lying on my back while a White man projecting no feeling whatsoever literally sucks and scrapes out the contents of my womb. It's about all of the women who sat in that clinic with me, including the sixteen-year-old Latina who was four months pregnant and said this would have been her third child. All the women who do not make enough money, do not feel they have the support—financial, emotional, psychological, or otherwise—or the desire to bring new life into this world. It's about me not being able to write about this experience until age twenty-two, when I transferred to U.C. Berkeley and found myself with June saying, "Speak the truth. Be Poet."

The day I read the poem "Abortion Flashbacks" to the class, I held my breath and took the long dive to say the words.

> oh god
> must i watch hear feel
> incessant scraping

metal against flesh

my uterus screams

contracting wildly in confusion…

I had never shared this experience, or any experience this personal, with people I had only known for a few weeks. Revelations. I was not the only one crying when I finished. A young woman across from me said that she had never heard someone write about abortion in that way.

A beginning. The list of words that aches to be shared unfolds continuously, each layer bringing me closer and closer to the Center. As personal as poetry can be, you are never speaking only for yourself. For example, I write for my younger brother whom I remember as a playful, smiling, easy-to-laugh, easy-to-cry young man before the age of twelve. Now my brother, very tall, very Black, and very handsome, still smiles with friends and family, but he does not smile at White people that he doesn't know because he has learned that he is considered dangerous, a criminal, the enemy. And he doesn't smile at brothers on the street that he does not know because, as statistics of Black-on-Black crime show, they too could be his enemy. Instead he makes direct eye contact, nods, and perhaps says, "Whut'ssup?" And he never cries anymore. "

How does it feel to be considered both dangerous and an endangered species? How does it feel to be followed around in stores by suspicious salespeople, stopped on the street, searched, and interrogated by cops for no reason, or avoided by White people at night? Does it make you mad?" In answer to these questions he merely shrugs and replies matter-of-factly, "You get used to it." I listen between his words and I write because I know that he isn't used to it. I know it like I know my anger as an African American woman who loves all three of her brothers deeply. I know that this is the brother who tries to conceal his hurt at any mention of "Daddy," who contracted leukemia and joined the ancestors four years ago. My brother will say, "I don't want to talk about it, Kelly." But poetry will ripple from within the deep black pores of his skin and I will write it.

[handwritten margin note: black men are not animals.]

[handwritten margin note: "You Get used to it…"]

Everyday a poet is on the front lines. A poet does not live in one place. A poet lives in Somalia, Bosnia, Haiti, Cuba, Mexico, and East Oakland. A poet is like my great-great grandmother walking through the mountains of Asheville, North Carolina, calling out the sick, finding the proper plants, and then healing. A woman who knew that if you don't pay attention to what's hurting you, like, for instance, a blister on sore feet, it will fester until you can't walk no more and Lawd knows you got to walk cuz we still got a long long way to go.

Kelly Navies
(photo by June Jordan)

Kelly Elaine Navies *writes, "Like the Banjo, I was stolen from Africa—but the middle passage did not break my strings nor destroy my song." She lives, writes, and teaches in Oakland, California.*

Margaret Hiller: A Poet in Her Own Right   Elizabeth Riva Meyer

My mother kept an 8-1/2" x 11" photo of her mother on her nightstand near
her bed. The woman in the frame dictates strength with the serene yet proud
focus of her eyes. My sister and I would ask from time to time, "Who's that
woman in the picture?" and my mom would answer, "That's my mother. She
passed away, she was very sick." As a young girl, I knew nothing about this
woman, except that she was one of the most beautiful women I had ever seen
and that she had become sick and died.

When my mom told me about her mother's suicide, we were in the car
going down Poplar Avenue in Memphis. It was very hot outside so it must have
been summer. The bank clock with huge digital numbers flashed on the right-
hand side. Seessel's Grocery was on the left, and we pulled over to the photo
store on the right to continue talking. I felt sad and strange. I became
immediately aware of my grandmother, close to me. This woman had created
a family. She had made decisions. She had killed herself. And I needed to
know why.

Poetry allowed me to delve into that question even though I was writing
about a family secret. One voice inside me said I had no right to speak of my
grandmother, while another voice told me to write.

As I began working on my poem "For Margaret," my grandmother came
alive for me. I imagined the car she drove, the style she wore her hair, the way
my grandfather watched her and, at the same time, I inquired into what
forced her to choose death. I rejected the idea that my grandmother was
"mentally ill."

If my grandmother's truths could have been heard, if she could have
spoken her poetry, perhaps she would have survived. I imagine this woman
finding refuge in a poem. I imagine her inside a small brick house on a quiet
street in Memphis, with the noise in her head growing, directing her into the
back room. I see myself as friend and guide. Clasping her hand into both of
mine, I read poetry. I recite words of poets who have healed me: Joy Harjo,
Judy Grahn, June Jordan, Lucille Clifton, Sharon Olds, Pablo Neruda, and
Yusef Komunyakaa. I feed her. I channel life into her, and we begin a
relationship, allowing all of our voices to speak.

Like genetic chemistry, voices trickle down blood lines. They create
dialogue inside grandchildren. Listening to that dialogue, I collect stories to
write poetry.

I wrote "For Margaret" not only as a gift to my grandmother—a return of
respect and a surge of life—but also as a personal revolution against "soul
death" and a commitment to live with voices.

25

from *For Margaret*   Elizabeth Riva Meyer

down in the living room
under baby photos and kindergarten documents
a newspaper clipping
sketches the end of Margaret Hiller's life
some day in August
summer in Memphis
near the bridge
next to her car.

i know this woman
who left her husband
two daughters and the everyday ritual
of housewife gone mad.
in the newspaper clipping
Mr. Hiller carves
an image for the press
excluding himself
because "she was a sick woman."

i read the clipping
flash back and forth to her picture
so gentle and demanding
and i do not believe in sickness.
i see a woman
who jumped off a bridge
because the water below her flew fast and
her life dragged too slow
because the sick people who shared this bridge with her
made her a passerby, a woman of nothing
a woman.

i wish to see Margaret
that day in August
summer in Memphis
on the bridge
as she stops only to look at the water
below her fast and furious with speed
and in agreement drives west.

i hope that her death proves nothing
to the doctors and the other useless strangers
i wish to cure this history of sickness
which hovers over my family
which watches its sisters and mothers
leap from bridges
because these women keep cities alive
despite the recurrent lie
of suicide as a remedy.

Elizabeth Meyer with Sazi.
(photo courtesy of Elizabeth Meyer)

Elizabeth Riva Meyer *laughs loudly, grooves to any music which moves her body, dreams of riding horses, and continues to investigate the complexities of being born a Southern girl.*

Crouching in the Shadow of Columbus's Tomb   Shanti Bright

I stood in front of Columbus's tomb in Seville, Spain, menstruating, a twenty-year-old mixed-blood woman, a student, and an American tourist. Candles illuminated some of the Gothic cathedral, but its dark enormity overpowered the small lights. The gray floors and gray tomb exuded a stale chilliness. As I stared and wandered among the endlessly high columns guarding the tomb, my mind raced through all the moments leading to this one. I wanted to understand the amazing and tragic confluences and coincidences in my life, to make sense of my blood and the life and death of Columbus, the genocide of Native Americans and the strength of my family. But I was overwhelmed in the maze of connections.

Many of my stories cross paths with stories of Columbus. My grandmother, a half-Creek Indian from Oklahoma, survives generously. She has sewn me sixty pairs of pants and delicately embroidered my name on overalls. She bakes me my favorite peach cobbler and tells me stories of herself as a basketball star. She's my example of an Indian woman. My father fights for the old ways; a linguist and artist, he works to revive the Muscogee language. The death and chaos Columbus brought to this continent sometimes consume him. His struggle has taken him far from me at times. But he carves me pipestone bears and he likes to give me vitamins. My mother has given me all of her. She survived the destruction of her parents from alcohol, and taught me to plant a garden. I remember that she cried when I got my first period. I yearn to live as strong as she, to laugh loud and bold in the face of debt and suicide and loneliness.

I search for the meaning of my place among these stories in university classes, poems, endless journal entries, papers, football games, and powwows. I also travel. In high school I went to Costa Rica. It was green and lush, its people proud that only a few Indians still lived there. In college I went to Spain, searching for help with my identity questions. Like many other tourists, I ended up in the cathedral several times, staring at the iron tomb. The tomb became the focal point for the connections I was making.

When I returned to Berkeley my senior year, I began writing an honors thesis about the issues of tribal enrollment, mixed-blood identity, the history of patriarchal domination and Native women. But I knew a term paper could not express my own connections to these issues as powerfully as a poem. I returned my focus to the tomb. A poem begins with an image, and none seemed as poignant as my crouching next to Columbus's enormous tomb.

I began to combine notes from journals, letters home, and scribbles on napkins. I worked on the poem with my writing group and revised it several

times. Still, it did not feel complete until I read it publicly, on campus, to a
crowd of hundreds of sweaty people. When the audience listened, I began to
make more connections. That fall, Poetry for the People presented its semester
of writing under the theme, *Poetry in A Time of Genocide*. Our proceeds
benefitted groups that aided Bosnian women and children, victims of ethnic
cleansing. In that context, my poem became more than a private catharsis.

"Poetry in a Time of Genocide."
(Artwork by Hal BrightCloud)

Crouching in the Shadow of Columbus's Tomb   Shanti Bright

In the largest Gothic cathedral in the world
Sevilla, España
Four, twenty-foot, iron giants
Protect his remains
From crazed Indian women   like me
Young poets obsessed
with the man: like me
Inspiration and destruction   of me.

I shrink in the shadow of the tomb
My Spanish companions kiss
the cup he drank from
Admiration whispers whirl
Faint and nauseous
I think my life
Led me to this moment with him   here.

In Costa Rica
I discovered the rich coast   like him
Ignorant   like him
of what was to come.
Now in Spain where he departed
I long to hold a dark woman in my arms   like him
to ignore his bloody hands.

My grandmother survived
From her a woman in me
Fights,
fists up and brutal,
Against the Columbus in me.

I want to dive
Through steel
Touch ashes
Know his death
Find answers…

Why did you throw my grandmothers down?
Why did you bring disease?
Why did you give guns?
Why did you leave a legacy so thick and suffocating
My father cannot breathe?

Why do I follow you?

501 years later
I crouch in the dank church
Menstruating,
Struggling for connections and poems
Womaness and nativeness
In the country where you began my destruction.

Shanti Bright
(photo by June Jordan)

Shanti Bright *loves mangoes and the poetry of Joy Harjo. She finished her Senior honors thesis, and graduated from Uuniversity of California at Berkeley in May, 1994.*

My-Linguality   Ananda Esteva

My preschool teachers forbade me from participating in group activities when
I spoke in Spanish. One teacher told me ants would fly in my mouth if I didn't
speak English. I spent so long with my tongue in my pocket, I forgot I could
talk. They wanted me to speak just like them so I shut up.

We had just moved to San Francisco from Chile. On Sundays, we opened
the door joining our apartment with our Mexicano neighbors and threw big
dancing parties. We spoke Spanish with our friends—refugees from
Guatemala, Argentina, and El Salvador. I remember smelling black beans
boiling in pots bigger than me while hearing salsa y cumbia rhythms and feet
shuffling across the linoleum floor. Mama sang with el Argentino, Valenzuelo.
She had worked with the leftist/art community in Chile, where she sang
strong folk songs through the night and day with her comaradas.

After a while, the parties stopped. We quit talking about our times back in
Chile. We ignored the growing dolor we held in our chests. Too many of my
parents' friends had been tortured.

The newspapers said they "were disappeared." Isn't that a safe phrase, "to
be disappeared," as though it occurred magically when, in fact, the
disappearances were calculated. Intending to erase the voices of el pueblo,
the Chilean government dragged people from their homes and killed them—
made them "disappear."

I missed Mama's voice and the golpes she struck on the guitar. As I grew
older, I felt sure she'd lost these songs, that they'd dried up dead, just as I'd
lost my native tongue. I didn't expect to conjure up their spirits again, but
when Poetry for the People demanded we write from urgent moments and in
our own languages, I began to write myself home.

I sat in my cheap closet-room trying to recapture the part of me with
something to say. I started rummaging my brain for memories but they all
seemed dumb. Then I threw my favorite records onto the turntable, the ones
we brought from Chile. Atahualpa Yupanqui's song "El Aromo" seeped out of
the speakers and invoked shivers in my body. I sang loud as I could, holding
tight to the spirit thundering through that song. I started to remember the
stories my parents used to tell me of how I came to be: how my mama lost
hope after the doctors forced forceps and experimental drugs into her body,
how fear snatched her voice when she lost her water two months early. I
knew I had to write a poem to remind her how strong she is.

My song-poem, called "Mama If You Only Knew Your Strength," weaves in
vital strands of Atahualpa's song. It tells how my Mama would sing his words
as she walked along the water's edge searching for strength and place.

Mama, If You Only Knew Your Strength!   Ananda Esteva

Some nights / she'd walk along the water
and sing the songs of Atahualpa Yupanqui.
Hay un Aromo nacido   (an aromo bush is born
en la grieta de una piedra   from the crack of a rock
parece que la rompió   it appears that it broke her
por salir adentro de ella   passing through)

Her first child / melted in the heat.
Gloved, White hands dug into her
like overworked miners / full of brisk and business
to rid her of the body.

Full moons of yellow death / called hepatitis
shrouded my Mama
the Meica, the Shaman / starved
and the doctors wouldn't touch her then.
Such a long winter within her belly.
The neighbors left food by the door on Sundays
Papi boiled eucalyptus leaves / but my brother / didn't breathe.

After her fever died
doctors labeled her a dust-bowl,
plowed by forceps / dry through drought.
With regal script / Doctors claimed her land infertile.
She relived the colonial songs of
women caught between
the old way and the new.
La pericona se ha muerto   (The woman died.
no pudo ver a la Meica   She could not see the Shaman.
Le faltaba su milcao   Missing her milcao—her payment—
por eso, se cayó muerta.   she fell dead.)

The tantrums of the winter ocean
cracked rocks against the cliffs
until Spring set in
and so did I.
No one knew I lived.
I hung strong like kelp / withstanding storms of blood and fear.
Two bleeding cycles passed by me / while the medics read her rights.
She thought she owned
only
half a body.
She cried along the water's edge / many mornings too.
She threw my brother's ashes there.
She thought
her thirsty body crumbled there.
Mama, if you only knew your strength
perhaps
today
you'd dance.

Ananda Esteva
(photo by Samiya Bashir)

Ananda Esteva *just started speaking up for herself and hopes her voice will carry
her far. She is a Film Studies major and works for Nicaragua Medical Aid.*

2

BUILDING A COMMUNITY OF TRUST WITHIN A POETRY WORKSHOP

GUIDELINES FOR CRITIQUING A POEM: THE POETRY DISTILLER

Long after I was reading and writing poetry with the same regularity as my a.m. cup of coffee, I became a teacher. Suddenly, I had to explain why a poem "worked" or why a line, or a verb, was "weak." I needed to devise an explanation that would hold, regardless of the content, or structural style, of the poem. I found specific guidelines for specific schools of contemporary poetry. But I could never find one set of rules that every serious poet could embrace as valid. Very tentatively, I began to compose that missing set of rules.

Over a period of four or five years I tested them, and my students challenged them, as well. At last, this exploration produced ten guidelines that no variety, or purpose, of a poem could usefully defy, or ignore. Miraculously, it was a fact: if you adhered to "The Guidelines" your poem enjoyed a better than ever chance of standing as A Good Poem. Certainly, whatever you wrote would gain greater force and singularity.

—June Jordan

June Jordan's Guidelines for Critiquing A Poem

1. Read it aloud.

2. Is it a poem?
   a. Poetry: A medium for telling the truth.

   b. Poetry: The achievement of maximum impact with a minimal number of words.

   c. Poetry: Utmost precision in the use of language, hence, density and intensity of expression.

3. What is its purpose?

4. Is it coherent?

5. What are the strengths of the poem?

6. What are the weaknesses of the poem?

7. Is it a good poem?
   Technical Checklist:
   a. Strong, descriptive verbs. Eliminate all forms of the verb "to be."

   b. Singularity and vividness of diction

   c. Specificity/resonant and representative details

   d. Avoidance of abstractions and generalities

   e. Defensible line breaks

f. Compelling/appropriate horizontal and/or vertical rhythm and/or vertical line breaks (See June Jordan's essay on vertical rhythm.)

g. Alliteration/Assonance/Dissonance

h. Rhyme

i. Consistency of voice/distance from the reader/diction

j. Dramatic inconsistences

k. Punctuation (Punctuation is not word choice. Poems fly or falter according to the words composing them. Therefore, omit punctuation and concentrate on every single word. E.g., if you think you need a question mark then you need to rewrite so that your syntax makes clear the interrogative nature of your thoughts. And as for commas and dashes and dots? Leave them out!)

8. Is it complete? Is it a dramatic event? Does it have a beginning that builds to a compelling middle development and then an ending that "lands" the whole poem somewhere fully satisfying to the reader?

9. How does it fit into or change a tradition of poems?

10. Read the poem aloud!

Repeat your critical passage through these guidelines.

THE GUIDELINES IN ACTION

In the following pieces, June and student poets discuss how and why the guidelines help to clarify and animate their work. Vertical rhythm is perhaps the most difficult element of the guidelines to grasp. (Most of us are still reaching!) We encourage you to read June's poem and her explanation of it aloud.

More Than You Ever Wanted To Know
About Vertical Rhythm   June Jordan

In traditional Western poetry, the rhythmical organization of words has been measured in relationship to the horizontal line. The pattern of stressed and unstressed syllables discernible in a line of poetry has been analyzed in order to determine whether the line follows an iambic or a dactylic or an anapestic metrical arrangement. In the 1960s, we, black poets, developed a different kind of rhythmical stucture for poetry. I call it vertical rhythm. Rather than depending only upon a distribution of stressed and unstressed syllables in a line, the rhythmical structure of black poetry depends upon the exploitation of musical qualities inherent to each word, and existing between and among words as well. Assonance or alliteration, for example, can produce a smooth movement from one word to another, from one line to another, and can even propel a listener or reader from one word or one line to the next without possible escape. Conversely, exploitation of musical devices such as dissonance inherent to, and discoverable between and among, words can slow or stop the movement from one word to the next or from one line to the next. Typically, the use of vertical rhythm will exploit the positive musical value of words (e.g. assonance or alliteration) in order to speed the reader all the way to the conclusion of the poem, and in order to make the reader's progress through the poem a pleasurable rhythmical experience. In addition, vertical rhythm— the propelling of the reader/listener from one line to the next—can be accomplished by manipulation of syntax.

Examples of Components of Vertical Rhythm
from *Free Flight*

June Jordan

1	Cheddar Cheese disintegrating luscious
2	on the top while
3	mildly
4	I devour almonds and raisins mixed to mathematical
5	criteria or celery or my very own sweet and sour snack
6	composed of brie peanut butter honey and
7	a minuscule slice of party size salami
8	on a single whole wheat cracker *no salt added*
9	or I read Cesar Vallejo/Gabriela Mistral/last year's
10	complete anthology or
11	I might begin another list of things to do
12	that starts with toilet paper and
13	I notice that I never jot down fresh
14	strawberry shortcake: never
15	even though fresh strawberry shortcake shoots down
16	raisins and almonds 6 to nothing
17	effortlessly
18	effortlessly
19	is this poem on my list?
20	light bulbs lemons envelopes ballpoint refill

Line 1: **Cheddar Cheese disintegrating luscious** displays two sets of musical relationships: **Ch** and **Ch** and the **s** sounds in disintegrating and luscious. Then from line 1 **luscious** to line 2 **on** provides for an elision so that the sounds move you, without space or breath, from **luscious** to **on**.

Line 2: **while** and **mildly** (line 3) display a relationship of assonance (**i** and **i**) and of alliteration, the (**i-l** and **i-l** sounds) so that you move happily from line 2 to line 3.

> 2   on the top while
>
> 3   mildly

Line 4: The first word **I** picks up the **i** sound in the only word of line 3, thereby connecting both the lines inescapably.

> 4   I devour almonds and raisins mixed to mathematical
>
> 5   criteria or celery of my very own sweet and sour snack

Lines 4, 5 and 6: These lines are interconnected by the device of alliteration carried by a last word to a first, e.g. **mathematical** and **criteria**.

Lines 6 and 7: These lines are connected by the manipulation of syntax: Line 6 conveys a random and excessive number of items. The last word **and** underscores the piled-up quality of the snack but also, syntactically, leads you into line 7 where the pile of items continues to build.

> 6   composed of brie peanut butter honey and
>
> 7   a miniscule slice of party size salami

Line 7: The **s** sounds cohesify this line, and the last word, **salami**, slides nicely into the first part of line 8 **on a single**. The compelling sound relationship between the two lines is further buttressed by the additional alliteration created by the **l** in **salami** and the **l** in **single**.

> 8   on a single whole wheat cracker *no salt added*

Line 8: Ending the line with **no salt added** necessarily slows or stops the reader because you cannot say **added** fast. This slowing down serves to control the reader's pace just prior to a change signalled at the start of line 9 by the word **or**:

> 9   or I read Cesar Vallejo/Gabriela Mistral/ last year's

Line 9: This line exploits **s** and **l** sounds for its cohesion. Furthermore the line exploits the **s** and **l** sounds of its last two words. Syntactical manipulation speeds the reader into line 10's first two words:

10   complete anthology or

Line 10: This line joins with line 11 by means of the conjunction **or** (a
syntactical manipulation):

11   I might begin another list of things to do

Line 11 and line 12: These lines are joined by dint of the hinged sense of
the two lines (syntactical manipulation) plus the alliteration between **things
to do that**.

Lines 12 and 13: These lines are joined by means of the conjunction **and**
(syntactical manipulation of words on different lines) and by exploiting the
alliterative recurrence of the consonant **t** (**starts/toilet/notice/jot**).

12   that starts with toilet paper and
13   I notice that I never jot down fresh

Line 13: The last word, **fresh**, elides with the first word of line 14,
strawberry, by exploiting the assonant and alliterative relationships between
fresh and **straw**.

14   strawberry shortcake: never

Line 14: The last word, **never**, elides with the first word of line 15, **even**.

15   even though fresh strawberry shortcake shoots down

Line 15: This line revels in **s** and **sh** sounds. The last word, **down**,
syntactically compels you to the first word of the next line: **Raisins**.

16   raisins and almonds 6 to nothing

Line 16: The last word, **nothing**, elides with the first and only word of line
17:

17   effortlessly

Line 18: Repetition of **effortlessly** underscores its emphatic, rhythmical
function. Also, the last syllable of **effortlessly** elides with the first word of the
last line (line 19) **is.**

18   effortlessly

Line 19: The poem comes to a dramatic moment requiring that the reader
either slow down or stop. The line compels the reader to do so by exploiting
the dissonant effect of the last two consonants of the word **list**, which also has

an assonant relationship with the earlier words, **is** and **this**: <u>is this</u> **poem on my list?**

19   is this poem on my list?

Line 20: After the slowdown of line 19, line 20 speeds up the reader by relying heavily upon the alliteration among the words full of **l** sounds:

20   **lightbulbs lemons envelopes ballpoint refills.**

Et cetera.

Junichi P. Semitsu,
student teacher poet,
Spring 1995.
(photo by June Jordan)

In the essays below, Gary uses the Guidelines to prune his poem into shape, and Shelly Teves offers a philosophical/personal/political endorsement of the guidelines.

Vujà-dé   Gary Chandler

I should say, first of all, that before last semester I had never written poetry. This poem was only the third poem I wrote, and the first I seriously critiqued. Sitting down with my poem and June's Guidelines, I felt heavy "Vujà-dé"—the feeling that this had never happened to me before. Here's my first draft:

Untitled First Draft

Wet tongues of heat
slobber on the city
panting gasping licking
unleaving leaving
smears of liverwurst smog
in my lungs cheeks armpits

Noise overflows its banks in my head
flooding the valleys of my mind
gushing through
my ears nostrils eyelids mouth
pooling in the hollows
where I have lost my concentration
muddy puddles breed mosquitoes
whose swollen bites
itch
unscratched unscratchable
even by
naiveté's narrow fingers of
adaptability

This place where I live breathe exist
loiters like a chewed-up lump of meat
in my small intestine
undigested indigestible

the women men (someone's child?) on the corner
mix with stomach acid
and the burrito from the market where
jingle-pocketed
I apologized lied
"Sorry I don't have any"
and felt so good liberal stupid
but kept on walking
anyway.

It wilts like the rotten banana
in their refrigerator
in your garbage can
in my pants
stinking like trails of diarrhea
unwiped unwipeable
by double pleated perforated squares
of "tolerance."

In this place
I exist amidst
eyes always spying
voices always blaring
lights always glaring

I feel dissected
the expression on a stiff cat's face
unseen unseeable
unknown unknowable

Revising this poem, I started with what stuck out most—the lists, like *panting gasping licking* and *live breathe exist.* Guideline #2 says poetry achieves "maximum impact with minimal number of words" and it uses "precision of language." When I thought about it, listing words goes against both of these. One word is more "minimal" and "precise" than three. A list of words can work if each word adds dramatically to the next, and if together they contribute to an "overall" expression. It can also help rhythm. My lists were just wordy.

Moving right along, I went to the first stanza. Inconsistent metaphors everywhere. As I see it, they're double whammies, since they stem from an imprecision of words (guideline #2) and make the poem hard to follow (guideline #4). I'm not really sure *what* connection I intended to make between *slobbering wet tongues* (dog imagery) and *liverwurst* (deli imagery?). A poem should hold together. If it feels disjointed, perhaps there is more than one poem in there. In the second stanza, my metaphorical sizing, so to speak, was off. Would a noise *overflowing* and *gushing,* leave *puddles* (as I wrote), or would it leave *lakes*?

Cutting away wordiness and dead images helped me answer guideline #3: "What is the purpose?" Excessive words can obscure the purpose of a poem, even from the poet. A clear sense of purpose helps me distill my meaning and communicate forcefully. I realized, finally, that I wrote this poem as a response to the word *tolerance,* and the indifference it implies. Understanding this, I pared away even more.

Sad to say, my first reaction to my revisions was distinctly negative: The poem had lost its heart. It felt fragmented and incohesive. I found editing can make a poem lose (or appear to lose) that first-draft feeling of raw *truth.* What saved me were the guidelines, especially number three: purpose. Whenever in a bind, think again about why you wrote the poem in the first place. Sticking to the guidelines, I went through five more revisions and, ultimately, settled on the sixth as "final."

Another important piece of advice came from poet Marilyn Chin, who gave a lecture on Asian American poetry in our spring 1994 class. She said, "You have to love your poem more than you love yourself." She meant that a poet must hold the quality of the poem in greater regard than his or her personal affection for particular words, lines, or stanzas. Initially, I clung to certain words and phrases like *hollow dusty corners/where I have lost my concentration,* even though they didn't contribute to the poem's purpose. To move forward, I had to decide that the poem must come first.

Even as I wrote this essay, I revised the poem further. Here it is, in its brand-new, "final" distillation.

Tolerance

city situations
loiter like a chewed-up lump of meat
undigested
in my small intestine

people on the street
mix with stomach acid
and burritos from the corner store where
jingle-pocketed
I
mister liberal
apologize
lie
"Sorry, I don't have any."

Robert Burnett, Gary Chandler,
Felicia Sze, and Harmony
Goldberg use June's Guidelines
for Critiquing A Poem to
scrutinize what to cut and what
to keep in their own work.
(photo by Ananda Esteva and
Samiya Bashir)

Gary Chandler *grew up in Kirkwood, California, where he spent most of his
Thanksgivings cutting kindling. He is majoring in Ethnic Studies at the
University of California, Berkeley.*

A Poem Lives

Shelly Teves

I live in a lie-encrusted culture where carcinogenic fumes from aerosol cans pass for a "fresh clean scent," where "feminine hygiene" means toxic tampons, where the Rodney King trials pass for "justice." Searching for powerful expression infused with truth in our English speaking culture is like looking for healthy food in a 7-Eleven. The people in the "English Only Movement" are right when they say that the English language is in a state of decay. We cannot blame that decay on people who speak other languages. Nor can we blame the people who take English into their culture as a living thing that interacts, slaps skin, smiles and sings. On the contrary, the people who sit down to dinner with English bring about innovations that keep it alive and growing. Still, we all kill English every time we tell a lie. We subjugate it, force it to do our bidding and sever it from the truth. Even when we unintentionally obscure the truth, we strip the language of its power. English withers and dies. Now can you smell the rot of toxic shock syndrome or aerosol chomping on your cell walls or the acquittal of four L.A. police officers?

I wage a personal campaign to revitalize English. This campaign requires that I tell the truth. In order to become more honest, I must first come into consciousness about when, how, and why I lie. Sometimes I lie with intention. For example, "I don't have my paper because the computer erased my disk. I'll have to type it again." Other times my lies obscure the truth with abstraction, clichés, vague words and passive constructions. These are unintentional lies, bad habits from the way I was raised. For the first eight years of my life, I grew up on TV dinners, a delicious square meal, and Frosted Flakes, a nutritious part of a good breakfast. I grew accustomed to lies.

When some people hear about "Guidelines for Critiquing Poetry," they recoil from what strikes them as poetic fascism. They feel that even the idea of guidelines violates the sanctity of their instincts and sterilizes their personal truth. But the guidelines sharpened my instincts. I came to poetry through Poetry for the People. Since I had no preconceived notions about writing poetry, I did not have an internal philosophical conflict over using the guidelines. They helped me come into consciousness about my lies. They gave me a set of tools I use to rid my voice of these lies. They point out what I need to look for as I revise my poems line by line.

Shelly Teves *sucks down early morning fog as she sweeps the sweet-tasting spider webs from wooded trails with her running.*

In these last two pieces, Leslie Shown and Ananda Esteva use excerpts from
their poems to explain the guidelines on diction (#7b) and line breaks (#7e).

A Short Discussion of Diction

Leslie Shown

from *slow southern song*

> lyin in bed all by myself on one of those you know oh so
>   lazy sunday mornings
> wonderin bout how come i don't hear no sweet man
>   singing to himself in the
> kitchen while he makes me blueberry pancakes and puts
>   on the kettle for tea

from *trying not to slip on ice*

> I move slowly through the dark territory of loss
> edging off the map of love which knew your name
> stumbling backwards from your life
> the country I most longed to travel

In both of these poems, a woman is reflecting on the absence of her lover. Yet
the difference in diction, or style of speaking, in the two poems makes them
very different from one another. In the first poem, I use short and simple
words that roll off the tongue easily and create a sense of lightness. In the
second poem, I use line breaks and more complex words to create the sense
that this woman is choosing her words very carefully and slowly. Rather than
lightness, I want to convey mournfulness.

The consistency of a voice within a poem is an important part of making
the poem coherent, of making it tell a story. For example, if I tried to write a
poem in which a woman started out speaking the language of "slow southern
song"and then began to speak the language of "trying not to slip on ice," you
would probably end up wondering if the speaker had suddenly changed,
rather than experiencing the poem as a coherent event.

Leslie Shown *has degrees in English Literature and Environmental Science and
Policy. Her husband, her garden, her dog, and poetry are her passions.*

Just Another Note on the Significance of Line Breaks   Ananda Esteva

Together with rhythm and rhyme, line breaks separate poetry from prose. I thought seriously about line breaks when I wrote my poem, *Hermanita Mía, Hija De La Tierra*. I wanted to convey both specific and double meanings. This poem talks about my sister coming of age, sprouting breasts, and becoming unfortunate enough to be represented in billboards as a Latina sex symbol. When we discussed the following chunk of *Hermanita Mía* in my workshop group, we decided that line breaks carry weighty consequences.

First I experimented with breaking the lines this way:

> just another Latina
> sex-symbol

"just another Latina" as its own line suggests the subject of the poem is a casual commodity. It also stresses her race; the word, "Latina" gets the emphasis when I say the line out loud. The next line informs the reader she's also a sex symbol. Breaking the lines in this way sets up a parallel between the two ideas: "just another Latina," therefore, equals "sex symbol."

Then I broke the lines this way:

> Just
> another Latina
> sex-symbol

Having "just" on its own has a belittling connotation, like saying, "She's nothing more than." Placing "another" at the beginning of the next line puts the emphasis on "another" and implies she is one of many Latinas. It makes "another" mean "yet one more."

Finally I broke the lines:

> just another
> Latina sex-
> symbol

Having "just another" on its own makes the reader depend on the next line to find out "just another what?" It sets up anticipation and a rhythm that moves the reader from one line to the next. The second line, "Latina sex," repeats the rhythm (with the same number of syllables) and answers the question. It's Latina sex! This line division implies "Latina sex" might be different/more exotic than other sex. However, the next line is "symbol." So it's not just Latina sex we're considering, but Latina sex symbols or Latina sex as symbolic! Instead of climactic cymbals after the build-up of the preceding lines, we get stopped short. As a one-word line, "Symbol" punctuates the rhythm. It might even make the reader stop and think.

Poetry Should
Ride the Bus!
(photo by
June Jordan)

THE WORKSHOP PUZZLE: PUTTING IT TOGETHER

A Framework for Productive Workshop Discussion   Dorothy Wang

June's guidelines for critiquing poetry not only force us to write the tightest
poetry possible, but provide a framework for productive workshop discussion,
helping us to avoid conversations consisting solely of "I like..." or "I feel..."
responses. Don't get me wrong. Feelings and (dis)likes play an important role
in workshop discussion, but they must be grounded in the particular—specific
examples (of words, lines, images) and identifiable criteria for judging
whether a poem "works" or doesn't. These criteria mirror, indeed are often
synonymous with, the guidelines used in the writing process. We may resist
them, but they give sinew to our speaking and writing. How much more useful
for a poet to hear, "This line is weakened by an overload of redundant
adjectives" than merely, "I don't know...somehow I just don't like this line."
Needless to say, criticism should always be constructive, never mean-spirited.

But in the event that a little (or a lot of) mean-spiritedness does enter into
the picture, concrete criteria can help to defuse such charged situations—i.e.,
those in which others are left feeling uncomfortable, excluded, or even
violated. Such emotionally wrought scenarios often spring from a poet's
having made broad—usually negative—generalizations, assumptions, and/or
criticisms about an individual or group, characterizing solely on the basis of
race, sexual orientation, gender, and so on. Again, concrete counterexamples
pack a more potent punch than shouting, "I hate you and your lousy poem"
(or similar sorts of imprecisely expressed rage).

Of course, a certain level of tension in a poetry workshop is normal and to
be expected. Since students regard poems, unlike calculus problem sets, as
personal emanations of themselves, they naturally find it difficult not to "take
it personally." Nevertheless, there is a distinct difference of degree between
such normal touchiness and a level of discomfort that threatens to undermine
the functioning of the workshop. If the group can manage to stay together—
i.e., in the same room—as differences are explored and if tensions can exist
without preventing each person from speaking, the group may discover a new
space where conflicting opinions can co-exist with mutual respect.

Dorothy Wang, *a graduate student in the English department at U.C. Berkeley,
was the Teaching Assistant for June Jordan's Poetry for the People class in the
fall of 1994. She's planning to begin her dissertation on Asian American poetry
any minute now.*

from *Voice Talking Loud*   Ananda Esteva

Today my voice sings strong and
fragile like a newborn in the sun.
It scares me.
i'm singin alongside peers and poets
all of us talking loud
feeling unified, and alone.
i want to know
do we harmonize
like wolves
gathering together before the hunt
or scavenge like jackals
snarl and bite into each other at the throat?

Today my voice sings strong and fragile
like a newborn in the sun.
Tell me, do I sing alone?

The poets of *Poetry for
the People During a
Season of Love.*
(photo by unknown
passerby)

Workshop Nuts and Bolts

Creating a community of trust does not meld us into a harmonic conver-
gence, require us to censor one another, or make us color-blind, class-blind,
or gender-blind. We begin by structuring an environment where we can
expose volatile issues without attacking one another, and can sustain responsibility rather than denial. It takes more than arranging the chairs in a circle.

On the first or second day of class, we divide into groups of seven to ten
poets who will write and critique poems together the entire semester. Usually
the groups form randomly, by numbering off and then putting the "1"s or
"2"s together in the same group, for example. Occasionally, groups form
around specific interests. One spring several new poets decided to write in
Spanish together and to supplement the reading assignments by studying
revolutionary Latina/o poets such as Martivón Galindo, Roque Dalton,
Nicolas Guillen, Octávio Paz, Rosário Murillo, and Daisy Zamora. A few
other students interested in speaking and learning poetry in American Sign
Language also formed a group that met regularly outside of class.

The workshop groups usually meet for two hours after the class lecture,
and sometimes (depending on the zeal of the members!) for additional hours
at a cafe, someone's house, or on a sunny lawn. Two or three Poetry for The
People alumni, a.k.a. student teacher poets (STPs), facilitate each group. The
student teacher poets organize the workshop meetings, hold office hours,
and grade their students' midterm and final writing portfolios. In addition,
they complete all of the writing assignments and share them with their
workshop groups before submitting them to June.

The First Meeting: Set the Tone, Establish How
the Workshops Work

Because our workshop groups include a range of ages, ethnicities, cultural
histories, and personal paths, it is especially important to spend time at the
first meeting "breaking the ice" and learning more about each other. Most
groups break into pairs, chat, then introduce themselves to their newly-
formed collective. For their first group meeting, student teacher poets Ananda
and Sean brought in clumps of never-hardening clay to stimulate creativity
and silliness, and to give folks something to do with their hands. Shanti and
Betty's group went around the circle and discussed their "relationship to
poetry," how long they'd been writing it, and why they decided to try the
course. Renata and Seyyida brought in their own poems with the active verbs
changed to passive ones, and the group revised them together, discovering

the power packed into active verbs.

Right from the beginning, we go over the Ground Rules for Poetry for the People and make a commitment to listen to and respect one another. When poetry addresses personal and political truths, it is bold, sometimes difficult, and risky—particularly since we inevitably discover and name the differences among one another. One person's "truth" may make another person wince, or cringe. Because unspoken resentment might damage group spirit, we ask poets to speak up as problems arise. We also agree to keep all poems and discussions confidential; this means we don't repeat anything outside of the group, until or unless the poet gives us permission to do so. Clear communication, mutual respect, and encouragement are necessary for a poetry workshop to flourish.

We spend most of our workshop hours critiquing one another's poems. Each writer brings copies of his or her poem for the entire group. She or he reads the poem aloud, and others respond, using June's "Guidelines for Critiquing a Poem" to comment on what's good about the poem before saying what needs work. It's essential that we offer frank, constructive, and specific reactions. When we're in the hot seat, we try to listen attentively to all suggestions, and to respect the ideas of fellow poets.

A gathering after the Poetry for the People in a Time of Genocide student reading. (photo by Stephanie Rose)

3

REFLECTIONS ON TEACHING
Power Tripping, Responsibility,
and Authority

The Poetry for the People student teacher poet program appeared on the scene several years ago, born of student demand: far too many people wanted to learn to write poetry each semester for just one professor to handle. With the proclamation "Each one teach one!" June launched a program whereby new poets become teachers of poetry. Each spring semester, approximately ten new teachers work with sixty new poets to keep Poetry for the People moving, growing, and evolving.

After taking the Poetry for the People course at least once, and after working with June in a seminar on teaching and writing poetry, students may apply to become student teacher poets. They read and sign the job description and write a one to two page statement of purpose.

JOB DESCRIPTION: STUDENT TEACHER POET

- Treat all students with equal good will and consideration.
- Enable other students to become literate in contemporary poetry; read and discuss and criticize assigned poetry with students.
- Enable other students to become proficient in the composition and the criticism of their own poetry.
- Follow the Syllabus and the Guidelines; read aloud and discuss and criticize student poems.
- Commit to one hour a week to conference with students.
- Commit to regular group discussion and/or individual conferences regarding teaching problems and/or your own poetry.
- Amass a selection of five new poems that satisfy your own and the course's criteria for excellence, by the end of the semester.
- Provide written responses, and determine final grades, for other students' poetry.
- Help to make Poetry for the People an important, public success for yourselves and the other students by undertaking specific task responsibilities related to student/guest poetry readings, and an anthology of student poems.

JOB APPLICATION FOR STUDENT TEACHING IN POETRY FOR THE PEOPLE

1. 150–250 Word Statement of Purpose. What do you think is the purpose of teaching people how to write poetry? (Why poetry and not something else? What do you want to achieve?)
2. "I have read the Job Description and the Ground Rules for Student Teaching in Poetry for the People. I am able and willing to satisfy the requirements of the job and to adhere to the Ground Rules to the best of my ability."

Signature:
Name:
Telephone Number:

WHY TEACH POETRY? (WHAT'S POWER GOT TO DO WITH IT?)

When we decide to teach Poetry for the People, we make a commitment to keep learning and listening. As the following pieces demonstrate, we arrive at the decision to teach from different trajectories.

Pamela Stafford, Spring 1995
Poetry for the People Teaching
Assistant and a motivational
force behind the Poetry for the
People program at Glide
Memorial Church.
(photo by June Jordan)

Why I Teach Poetry, or Young People Need to Know They Can Speak Pamela Stafford

In our society, words have tremendous power. When an individual can name her circumstance, name her pain, name herself, she becomes an active agent in her world. June Jordan taught me how to crack words open and let out the power. She forever changed my relationship with words. As a student in Poetry for the People, this knowledge transformed my life. The most important gift I can give to my students is to offer them the same opportunity. So many young people today have no words for the things they suffer, the things they fear. They need to know that they can speak to their circumstance in ways that will help them and others understand. They need what June Jordan gave to me: the ability to transform words into the truth, and speak them out to whomever will listen. As evidence of this, I offer my poem, "Standing Still."

Standing Still   Pamela Stafford

Stand still
Just a little longer
He says again.
A grown man, my own uncle
How could he…?
I don't even know the words
For a touch renamed invasion
I stand, and stand shaking
His fingers and tongue
Every where in me
they can be.

I hold protest inside
knowing the answer to:
Please I can't any more
It hurts let me go
The answer's the same:
I love you, my favorite
my doll, my living doll
so small I'LL TELL YOUR
MOTHER YOU NASTY GIRL
SHE WON'T BELIEVE YOU
YOU LIKE IT YOU KNOW YOU
LIKE IT

I shut my eyes tight
Tomorrow, a birthday cake,
Ten candles, a lavender dress
with a million petticoats to float it,
a coconut cake and presents and
And…IT HURTS!

Do you love me?
Say you love me.
I'll stop if you say it.
Say it again. Louder.

Then behind me around me over me
Hunched over, scrunched down to get
Inside a body so small, standing.
The pressing buckles my knees.
My lungs fill in agony and explode
A whisper IT HURTS!

Tears finally ease
My premature breasts back
Into their woman's bra.
Button my blouse so neatly.
Disjoin his body from mine
Smooth my skirt, turn me around
and fill my mouth with his tongue,
My ears with his whispers.

So good you are so good you are
such a good girl. My living doll.
Savaging fingers wipe my tears
You are so good you are…
When you can finish
I'll let you lay down and
do it like a big girl.

And he leaves me
Standing still.

Pamela Stafford *graduated Phi Beta Kappa from the University of California at Berkeley. She is currently pursuing a Ph.D. in English, and is the mother of two children.*

*From Shelly Teves's Application to Become a Student Teacher Poet
(which June accepted even though it exceeded the word limit)*

Shelley Teves

We rode like cargo, up to the Yuba River in the back of a four-cylinder pick-up colored like an aged canary. Lex lay as limp as lettuce, hungover and overheated in the swelter of early September. I stroked her hair and held out water, urging her to drink. We had a squat plastic jar filled with fat chunks of ice that slid into water across the skin on her forehead. I asked her if she wanted me to read to her and she said yes. So I dug in my pack and fished out a thin black volume, titled *Diving into the Wreck*.

I had never really read poetry before and I wasn't much used to reading out loud. I stumbled and stuttered through the stanzas of the first several poems, but I stuck with it. No, it stuck to me and smoothed itself out. "Wow," I said, as sunshine pressed upon me, making me sweat on the nylon sleeping bags.

After hiking, swimming, and sleeping, I awoke to swim again. With the sun high overhead, I placed my hands flat on the smooth, slippery rock and slid myself softly out of the water. I tugged off my wet shorts, ate a little lunch, then sat back to rest, digest, and read. Cradled on a stone couch under a moss-coated tree, I got sucked in by the images, moved by the rhythm, rattled by the power and anger.

I dove into the wreck from cover to cover and when I finally reached the surface, I found myself in the middle of an ocean licked by lightning and battered by thunder. Lex came back to find me surly and unable to speak coherently. She finally coaxed me back into the water where I found myself again.

"No more Adrienne Rich for you," she said.

I tell you this story because it is the truth and it has a lot to do with why I want to teach Poetry for the People. Over the past several years I have grown rather numb. For a long time, only dancing and swimming could thaw the chill of my exterior. Reading Adrienne Rich on the banks of the Yuba took a sledge hammer to a soul encased in ice. I became so terribly confused because I had no idea that poems could affect me like that, especially when I didn't always understand what they meant in any kind of rational way. Since then, I've been reading a lot and aloud. Whenever I find something that moves me, I will read it to my friends. I'll call my mother in Chicago or my father in LaSalle or my sister in New Mexico because I want to share with them. I delight in this.

I encountered poetry for the first time three months ago in Poetry for the People's Women's Studies course "Coming into the World Female." Even though I am a Religious Studies major, I have spent most of my nine semesters preparing for medical school, the career of my parents' choosing—a numbing experience in itself. Although I am no longer a registered student, I am submitting this application to teach poetry because I would love the chance to develop myself as a poet/person and to share my new-found fascination with others. I want to know if they feel the power, too—the power that comes from reawakening a sleeping soul.

Poetry has the power to rattle me with an alarm clock or to gently tug at my toe. So, in spite of Lex's order, I did not stop reading Adrienne Rich. In fact, one night I waited for my friend in a courtyard outside of her class. When she emerged, I immediately started reading "The Phenomenology of Anger." She quietly walked away. I followed her, still reading, breathing harder and heavier. She unlocked her bike and said, "A lot louder, please." So I climbed on the back and we rode out of the courtyard and down the hill, and all the way I shouted out the words on the page just as they were shouting out at me.

Temu Diaab, a student
teacher poet.
(photo by June Jordan)

TIPS FOR TEACHING POETRY WORKSHOPS

We try to remain vigilant about issues of power that arise in the context of teacher-student relationships: the power teachers assume to evaluate other people's work, the responsibility we take on as our students' guides to a new form of self expression, the muddy line between offering constructive criticism of their work and attacking them or their vision. As co-leaders of our workshop groups, we rely on one another for every aspect of this undertaking. Student teacher poets meet together on a weekly basis to consult June, her graduate student teaching assistant, and each other. We share success stories, develop new strategies and discuss teaching problems, whether the problems concern line breaks, student motivation, tension between students in our group, or grading issues. If we ever find ourselves facing a crisis too serious to handle within the structure of Poetry for the People (i.e. a threat of suicide or a complaint about sexual harassment), we rely on resources in the school or the community, such as psychological/counseling services, crisis centers/hotlines, or support groups.

The following pages provide specific teaching tips recommended by student teacher poets.

Claudia May, June's original
Poetry for the People Teaching
Assistant and a co-founder of
Poetry for the People.
Many thanks to Claudia for her
work and spirit.
(photo by June Jordan)

Tips for Facilitating a Poetry Workshop Discussion

1. Get to know everyone's name the first meeting.

2. Observe how your students learn; some thrive from other student comments, others may prefer to work one-on-one with an instructor.

3. After someone reads, wait for the other members of the group to respond before you do. Listen carefully to all responses. Encourage group members to do the same.

4. Have a ten- to fifteen-minute break during the workshop to allow an opportunity for poets to refresh their minds and to redirect the group into a new topic, if necessary.

5. HAVE FUN! Bring food and drinks to share during break. The communal sharing of food lets students socialize together and makes the job of a student teacher poet easier because the students feel more inclined to talk in the group.

6. Encourage students to bring *all* poems to *every* class meeting and to save all drafts of every poem. The group can compare old drafts to new ones, or return to a discussion from the previous week.

7. If one or two students do not get to read their poems aloud during the workshop, take those poems home and make suggestions. Return them the next class.

8. Rather than crossing out or editing a poet's work, write questions in the margins that will help him or her to revise it. The final decision is up to the poet.

10. Vary the routine. Read a poem from the assigned reading aloud and let everyone begin a poem in response to it. Break into pairs to exchange and critique work. Let group members read each other's work aloud, so that each poet can listen to how her or his poem sounds.

11. In the event of a distressing disruption by a member of the workshop, you might ask the person to stop expressing certain views or, *in extremis*, to leave altogether. "Hate speech" is the kiss of death for a poetry workshop.

Tips for Using the Guidelines for Critiquing A Poem

1. Establish the guidelines as a concrete reference point. Use them to offer constructive criticism.

2. Use the guidelines in concert with one another, not separately.

3. Limiting students to "one thought per poem" helps them to write one, fully coherent, satisfying, poem.

4. Help new poets revise abstract writing by asking them to describe their ideas or feelings in terms of what their five senses can understand: what it looks like, sounds like, tastes like, feels like, smells like.

5. If you don't understand what the poet is trying to do in a poem, ASK. Try to identify the source of confusion and discuss this with the poet.

6. When someone explains an unclear line or passage, jot down their explanation. Many times these explanations provide the key phrase or idea needed to illuminate the whole poem.

7. Ask students to bring in favorite poems from the reading assignments. Test them against the Guidelines. If a great poem seems weak in terms of one of the Guidelines (it uses the verb "to be," for example), determine what else in the poem allows the poet to get away with this lapse (good diction or rhythm, for example).

8. Encourage the group to critique your own (STP) work using the Guidelines. Ask questions like: "Does my purpose come across clearly? If not, where am I unclear?" "Does the diction change effectively when the speaker changes?" "Does the rhythm work?" "What do you think about the title?" "Do you believe me?"

9. Emphasize the need to *revise*. As June reminds us, "Once the poetry is out, you have to *worry* the lines."

10. Model the revision process. Bring in your own poems and demonstrate major structural changes. Bring in multiple drafts of poems published by established poets (generous guest poets provide a good resource here).

Tips for Office Hours

1. Meet with each of your students on an individual basis about every two weeks to discuss successes or problems with the course, individual poems, midterms or grades.

2. Ask students to bring their entire writing portfolio to office hours and to come prepared with specific questions.

Tips for Grading

1. At the beginning of the course, go over the grading policy as it is stated in the syllabus. Emphasize that we determine grades at the midterm and the end of the course, basing them on whether students complete all assignments, contribute positively to workshop meetings, and demonstrate improvement in their poetry.

2. Keep records of attendance and of all grades and summary comments.

3. Ask students to submit a written summary of their committee work helping with publication of the anthology and production of the readings and/or community outreach.

4. Consider returning the midterm or final poetry folders during individual conferences.

Tips on Inviting Guest Poets and Lecturers

To locate guest poets and lecturers, first check resources in your community and school. Get recommendations from your teachers. Ask managers of local book stores to sponsor a reading or book signing. Once guest lecturers agree to visit the class, you can arrange the date, send them a course description, and find out whether they want to assign particular readings. In addition, ask guest lecturers to bring a suggested reading list, which you can distribute to the class, and a curriculum vitae, which you can use to make a proper introduction. (For suggestions on making travel arrangements, see the section on Hot Shot Poets in Chapter 6.)

NAVIGATING THE HIGHS AND LOWS OF TEACHING

In spite of high hopes, creative tips and all kinds of resources, most teachers face frustration at some point in the semester. Below, Shanti describes one of the "breakthrough" moments that make it all seem worthwhile. Alegria reflects on team teaching, an activity which, at its best moments resembles dancing with an amazing partner, and, at its worst, feels like desertion or a bad date. Jin's reflective essay reminds us that as teachers, we are not the only ones responsible for the course's success or failure.

"Hey Listen"   Shanti Bright

Our workshop group included Irish, Mexican, Palestinian, African American, and Native American new poets. Marina wrote a poem about a man who claimed to be "female identified" and then sexually harassed her. She and I sat on a bench together one afternoon and talked about whether she should "go public" with her piece. She had written a powerful poem, but it scared her to say, out loud, "Hey listen! You cannot abuse me! You cannot abuse women anymore!" I told her I supported her, whatever she decided, but she remained uneasy.

Our conversation continued in our workshop. Everyone encouraged her. Some said, "Why write the poem unless you can tell the world about this jerk?" and, "Don't let him get away with this shit." Marina agreed her poem was not just about or for herself; she wanted to warn other women. She decided to publish the poem in the anthology. She even read it at our end-of-semester reading, speaking with a calm and steady voice. Eventually, every member of the group decided his or her poems would interest, move and speak to others. What Gonzalo says about homophobia in Mexico, and Tanika's discoveries about Blacks with Native American blood, and Renee's story about a young boy in a gang all create powerful connections when spoken, and demand action when heard.

Comments on Co-teaching   Alegria Barclay

The first day I walked into class as a certified Student Teacher Poet, I was terrified. I wouldn't even dream of teaching by myself. Co-teaching did eventually prove to be a blessing, but it had its sticky moments. I think the most difficult thing for us to learn was how to reconcile our personal poetic beliefs. My teaching partner, Xochi, followed the guidelines far more rigidly than I did. We didn't disagree on the guidelines on a basic level, but we differed on where the exception to the rule would lie. In deference to her adamant pleas to follow the guidelines religiously, I kept quiet, figuring it couldn't harm the students. The situation came to a head when one of our students, in class, asked if I agreed with Xochi since I never contradicted her. She said it would help them to know if I had another opinion on the matter. I was really surprised; it hadn't occurred to me that they might want more than one opinion, or that they would take my silence as compliance. I hadn't wanted to disrupt the class by undermining Xochi's authority. As it was, I did more harm. It was a better and far more comfortable approach for me to disagree with Xochi when I felt it was necessary. I learned that we could provide our students with two different views without confusing them, allowing them the choice to use the approach that best suited their poems.

Alegria Barclay soaking up the sun and editing tips from her poetry workshop group.
(photo by Ananda Esteva and Samiya Bashir)

Alegria Barclay *is half-Vietnamese, half-Caucasian. She is ever thankful to Xochi for her love, support and occasional moments of hysteria.*

Teaching, Trust, and Honesty

Jin Kyoung Jun

My experience as a student teacher poet this semester provided me with a different perspective on teaching. The enthusiasm, dedication, and growth exhibited by some students reaffirmed my own desires to enter the world of teaching. But the course also had a jarring effect. I came to realize that teaching isn't always about teachers helping their students, but about students who help themselves.

One of the most memorable aspects of teaching poetry was its veiled surprises. There were students who seemed to be gifted writers from the start; those who were content in their level of writing and, therefore, lacked enthusiasm; and those who never imagined they could write "real" poetry, but soared in spite of their fears. One of the latter students comes to mind. She had never taken a creative writing course in her life. Majoring in the sciences, she did not view herself as a writer, much less a poet. Her initial poems abided strictly by the guidelines for writing poetry and adhered to the structure of the assignments. They showed promise, but lacked vitality. After several weeks of individual meetings, intensive group workshops, disagreements, angst, and finally establishing a certain degree of trust and individual freedom, her writing took on new dimensions and meaning. An amazing thing happened: She began to bring a personal voice into her poems, rich with familial, cultural, and political resonance. She wrote eloquently of her childhood experiences of bigotry, the memories of her grandfather, and her sense of loss and separation from her Chinese people and land.

As her poetry continued to unfold, I began to reevaluate my role as a teacher in relation to the students. As a student teacher poet, I may have provided the guidance, support, and forum for her thoughts and words, but she, the student, had to struggle to find her own voice, listen to it, and tell us what it said.

During the semester, I became frustrated with another student who, despite my attempts to give him constructive criticism and "help," remained unreceptive to my suggestions. In fact, this student voiced his problems with our critiquing of his and other students' poetry. He had never taken a formal writing course, but had written on his own for years. He seemed intent to write and structure his poetry "his" way, in spite of problems with coherence, diction, rhyme, and abstractions. What initially appeared to be mere arrogance and resistance later took on a different shape—that of fear. I started to realize that perhaps he intended his poetry to remain vague. During office hours, he shared some of the feelings of fear and insecurity he claimed were behind the abstractions in his poetry.

By the end of the semester, after many unsuccessful attempts to get this writer to be more honest and specific in his poems, we required him to write two revisions (of his choice) that broke with his usual abstract images and monosyllabic rhymes. What he produced was something quite different. While there were still some problems, this new work displayed a degree of creativity, humor, and honesty not detected in his previous work.

From both of these relationships I learned that there is only so much a teacher can do. Offering students a challenge is one thing; having them face it and overcome it is another. This realization comes as a relief. Teachers don't need to be gods, saviors, or martyrs, and there are problems when they try or are expected to play those roles. People rarely meet up to the expectations created by themselves or others. This is good. Life should remain a constant striving toward expectations of improvement.

Jin Kyoung Jun at a Poetry for the People reading to protest Proposition 187. (photo by Bert McGuire)

Jin Kyoung Jun *treads the dangerous ground between literary criticism and liberation poetry. She is an undergraduate at the University of California at Berkeley.*

4

RESCUING THE CANON

Reinventing and Making it Relevant Again

What about the Canon?   Pamela Stafford

> The best thing that I can say about the canon is that it made sense of a way of
> thinking with which I was totally unfamiliar. Until that point it was impossible
> to reckon with a system I didn't understand. Once I understood this entire
> structure, then I knew what I could do to be recognized as myself.

An Indisputable Fact?   Shelly Smith

> What is the canon exactly? Does it exist in a vault somewhere at Yale? What
> does it have to do with us? Even when I did start hearing talk of the canon in
> school, I never really understood what it was exactly; the word always had this
> nebulous feel about it, not unlike the words "national interest" or "foreign
> policy" mouthed by politicians on the nightly news. As with those other terms, I
> understood that this canon thing affected my life in a way I could not grasp,
> and the strangest part about it was that professors talked about the canon as
> if it were a rock or a tree, an indisputable fact on the natural landscape of our
> education.

Untitled   Jamal Holmes

I am the neo-hoodlum intellectual
that alarms you so
the one just above the tides of poverty   but
just below the sands of the middle class

I study while I thieve   from you and yours
I break into your stuff
reciting shakespeare   and quoting socrates

educated in your institutions of granite pillars
and his story   and little white lies
but also   educated
in my institutions   of chain-link fences
and my story and   the black and white

the best and the worst
of two worlds   colliding
creating me: the neo-hoodlum
intellectual

the man in Black   with the briefcase
and intellectual glasses
that creeps around stealing
your forbes and newsweeks and your wall street journals

My accomplices and I
sit around the local liquor store
listening to chopin as we plot our next crime
after debating marxism with my brothers on the corner
I slide into the classroom and
debate the poetic value of tennyson

I steal and read and write and rob

I am the intellectual that charms you into leaving
your gates unlocked
then I become that hoodlum
that loots the
place
and leaves   you wondering   clueless

Jamal Holmes currently
reads, teaches, and writes
poetry in Los Angeles.
(photograph courtesy of
Jamal Holmes)

Creüsa*   Dorothy Wang

"O my sweet husband, is there any use/ in giving way to such fanatic
sorrow?…[Y]ou will reach/ Hesperia where…days of gladness lie in wait
for you:/ a kingdom and a royal bride." —*The Aeneid*, Book II

Trojan dame, you make me sick.
Unnatural as the yielding of broken toes
to gauze, your martyrdom warps me.
You weak woman, you.

Why spare your man fanatic sorrow
when the ages have not spared us,
wives and daughters? Palanquins trapped
nervous breaths and unfledged limbs.

But Aeneas—on him the Fates smiled
to found an empire, hook new brides,
and great glory, while for you they spun
a tangled thread of unglad days.

When we sigh, tears fall into
muddy water, buckets shouldered
swinging from the Yellow River. Not even
the Heavens turn an eye to the thinning.

How can I hear your cries when you yielded
your right, your place, your son? To you,
it was the gods' decree. Dido
dared to defy—for the privilege of snipping

her life's line by her own hand. In the end,
you two were tied like sisters, sharing
the same: a sacrifice—like countless Chinese
women praised in the name of honor

*First wife of Aeneas

and History. Now we, the daughters of Trojan
and Chinese women must learn to distill,
from their tears, clear spheres:
let Heaven thunder—what rain!—our songs.

Dorothy Wang, Poetry
for the People Teaching
Assistant, Fall 1994
and Donna Masini,
guest poet.
(photo by June Jordan)

CONTEMPORARY POETS TALK ABOUT THE CANON

In Poetry for the People, we have a lot of questions about the so-called literary canon. As new American poets, we consult guest poets and lecturers to help us name, reinvent, and reclaim literary and cultural traditions. Our guest speakers introduce us to the intricacies of not-yet-canonized histories and trajectories in poetry. For example, in a lecture on Caribbean poetry, VèVè Clark examined language and dialect in relation to culture and power in the works of Paul Keens Douglas and Derek Walcott. Commenting on Native American poetry, Maidu poet Janice Gould addressed the complexities of issues of translation, mixed cultural heritages, and the multiple forced removals of American Indian peoples. In a lecture on Chinese American poetry, Marilyn Chin acknowledged her indebtedness to Western poets like Keats, as well as to the Japanese haiku. Leroy Quintana opened our minds to the influence of the *corridos* on contemporary Chicana/o poetry. Dan Bellm looked to Emily Dickinson and Walt Whitman as predecessors of lesbian and gay poetic traditions. These guest presentations jump-start our pursuit of literacy in today's world literature of poetry.

In putting together this blueprint for Poetry for the People, we asked guest poets Adrienne Rich, Joy Harjo, Cornelius Eady, Marilyn Chin, Ntozake Shange, Leroy Quintana, Alfred Arteaga, and Janice Gould to answer questions about the canon. We wanted to know what works inspire them, whom they try to emulate, their relationship to the canon, and how they place themselves within specific cultural traditions. In the essay below, Adrienne Rich explains that even into her early adulthood she believed that "the poets in the anthologies were the only real poets." Certainly, many of us first learned about poetry in the way Rich describes. We believed that the relatively few, and almost exclusively male Anglo-Saxon poets were "inspired by some transcendent authority and spoke from some extraordinary height." Following Rich's inspiration, we hope to transform the canon that "embodies the naming and image-making power of a dominant culture." Joy Harjo's excerpt from "Talking to the Sun," and the generous, thoughtful comments sent to us by Eady, Chin, Shange, Bellm, Arteaga and Gould help us to move beyond the established canon, to open ourselves to new ways of knowing one another and ourselves.

from *Blood, Bread, and Poetry: The Location of the Poet*

Adrienne Rich

I was born at the brink of the Great Depression; I reached sixteen the year of Nagasaki and Hiroshima. The daughter of a Jewish father and a Protestant mother, I learned about the Holocaust first from newsreels of the liberation of the death camps. I was a young white woman who had never known hunger or homelessness, growing up in the suburbs of a deeply segregated city in which neighborhoods were also dictated along religious lines: Christian and Jewish. I lived sixteen years of my life secure in the belief that though cities could be bombed and civilian populations killed, the earth stood in its old indestructible way. The process through which nuclear annihilation was to become a part of all human calculation had already begun, but we did not live with that knowledge during the first sixteen years of my life. And a recurrent theme in much poetry I read was the indestructibility of poetry, the poem as a vehicle for personal immortality.

I had grown up hearing and reading poems from a very young age, first as sounds, repeated, musical, rhythmically satisfying in themselves, and the power of concrete, sensuously compelling images:

> All night long they hunted
>   And nothing did they find
> But a ship a-sailing,
>   A-sailing with the wind.
> One said it was a ship,
>   The other he said, Nay,
> The third said it was a house
>   With the chimney blown away;
> And all the night they hunted
>   And nothing did they find
> But the moon a-gliding
>   A-gliding with the wind....

> Tyger! Tyger! burning bright
>   In the forest of the night,
> What immortal hand or eye
>   Dare frame thy fearful symmetry?

But poetry soon became more than music and images; it was also revelation, information, a kind of teaching. I believed I could learn from it—an unusual idea for a United States citizen, even a child. I thought it could offer clues, imitations, keys to questions that already stalked me, questions I could not even frame yet: What is possible in this life? What does "love" mean, this thing that is so important? What is this other thing called "freedom" or "liberty"—is it like love, a feeling? What have human beings lived and suffered in the past? How am I going to live my life? The fact that poets contradicted themselves and each other didn't baffle or alarm me. I was avid for everything I could get; my child's mind did not shut down for the sake of consistency.

> I was angry with my friend,
> I told my wrath, my wrath did end.
> I was angry with my foe,
> I told it not, my wrath did grow.

As an angry child, often urged to "curb my temper," I used to ponder those words of William Blake, but they slid first into my memory through their repetitions of sound, the ominous rhythms.

Another poem that I loved first as music, later pondered for what it could tell me about women and men and marriage, was Edwin Arlington Robinson's "Eros Turannos":

> She fears him, and will always ask
>   What fated her to choose him;
> She meets in his engaging mask
>   All reasons to refuse him;
> But what she meets and what she fears
>   Are less than are the downward years,
> Drawn slowly to the foamless weirs,
>   Of age, were she to lose him....

And, of course, I thought that the poets in the anthologies were the only real poets, that their being in the anthologies was proof of this, though some were classified as "great" and others as "minor." I owed much to those anthologies: *Silver Pennies*; the constant outflow of volumes edited by Louis Untermeyer; the *Cambridge Book of Poetry for Children*; Palgrave's

Golden Treasury; the *Oxford Book of English Verse*. But I had no idea that they reflected the taste of a particular time or of particular kinds of people. I still believed that poets were inspired by some transcendent authority and spoke from some extraordinary height. I thought that the capacity to hook syllables together in a way that heated the blood was the sign of a universal vision.

Because of the attitudes surrounding me, the aesthetic ideology with which I grew up, I came into my twenties believing in poetry, in all art, as the expression of a higher world view, what the critic Edward Said has termed "a quasi-religious wonder, instead of a human sign to be understood in secular and social terms."[1] The poet achieved "universality" and authority through tapping his, or occasionally her, own dreams, longings, fears, desires, and, out of this, "speaking as a man to men," as Wordsworth had phrased it. But my personal world view at sixteen, as at twenty-six, was itself being created by political conditions. I was not a man; I was white in a white-supremacist society; I was being educated from the perspective of a particular class; my father was an "assimilated" Jew in an anti-Semitic world, my mother a white southern Protestant; there were particular historical currents on which my consciousness would come together, piece by piece. My personal world view was shaped in part by the poetry I had read, a poetry written almost entirely by white Anglo-Saxon men, a few women, Celts and Frenchmen notwithstanding. Thus, no poetry in the Spanish language or from Africa or China or the Middle East. My personal world view, which like so many young people I carried as a conviction of my own uniqueness, was not original with me, but was, rather, my untutored half-conscious rendering of the facts of blood and bread, the social and political forces of my time and place.

I was in college during the late 1940s and early 1950s. The thirties, a decade of economic desperation, social unrest, war, and also of affirmed political art, was receding behind the fogs of the Cold War, the selling of the nuclear family with the mother at home as its core, heightened activity by the FBI and CIA, a retreat by many artists from so-called "protest" art, witch-hunting among artists and intellectuals as well as in the State Department, anti-Semitism, scapegoating of homosexual men and lesbians, and with a symbolic victory for the Cold War crusade in the 1953 electrocution of Ethel and Julius Rosenberg.

Francis Otto Matthiessen, a socialist and a homosexual, was teaching literature at Harvard when I came there. One semester he lectured on five poets: Blake, Keats, Byron, Yeats, and Stevens. That class perhaps affected my

1. Edward Said, "Literature as Values," *New York Times Book Review* (September 4, 1983), p. 9.

life as a poet more than anything else that happened to me in college. Matthiessen had a passion for language, and he read aloud, made us memorize poems and recite them to him as part of the course. He also actually alluded to events in the outside world, the hope that eastern Europe could survive as an independent socialist force between the United States and the Soviet Union; he spoke of the current European youth movements as if they should matter to us. Poetry, in his classroom, never remained in the realm of pure textual criticism. Remember that this was in 1947 or 1948, that it was a rare teacher of literature at Harvard who referred to a world beyond the text, even though the classrooms were full of World War II veterans studying in the G.I. Bill of Rights—men who might otherwise never have gone to college, let alone Harvard, at all. Matthiessen committed suicide in the spring of my sophomore year.

Because of Yeats, who by then had become my idea of the Great Poet, the one who more than others could hook syllables together in a way that heated my blood, I took a course in Irish history. It was taught by a Boston Irish professor of Celtic, one of Harvard's tokens, whose father, it was said, had been a Boston policeman. He read poetry aloud in Gaelic and in English, sang us political ballads, gave us what amounted to a mini-education on British racism and imperialism, though the words were never mentioned. He also slashed at Irish self-romanticizing. People laughed about the Irish history course, said it must be full of football players. In and out of the Harvard Yard, the racism of the Yankee Brahmin toward Boston Irish was never questioned, laced as it was with equally unquestioned class arrogance. Today, Irish Boston both acts out and takes the weight of New England racism against Black and Hispanic people. It was, strangely enough, through poetry that I first began to try to make sense of these things.

"Strangely enough," I say, because the reading of poetry in an elite academic institution is supposed to lead you—in the 1980s as back there in the early 1950s—not toward a criticism of society, but toward a professional career in which the anatomy of poems is studied dispassionately. Prestige, job security, money, and inclusion in an exclusive fraternity are where the academic study of literature is supposed to lead. Maybe I was lucky because I had started reading poetry so young, and not in school, and because I had been writing poems almost as long as I had been reading them. I should add that I was easily entranced by pure sound and still am, no matter what it is saying; and any poet who mixes the poetry of the actual world with the poetry of sound interests and excites me more than I am able to say. In my student years, it was Yeats who seemed to do this better than anyone else. There were lines of Yeats that were to ring in my head for years:

Many times man lives and dies
Between his two eternities,
That of race and that of soul,
And ancient Ireland knew it all....

Did she in touching that lone wing
Recall the years before her mind
Became a bitter, an abstract thing
Her thought some popular enmity:
Blind and leader of the blind
Drinking the foul ditch where they lie?

I could hazard the guess that all the most impassioned, seductive arguments against the artist's involvement in politics can be found in Yeats. It was this dialogue between art and politics that excited me in his work, along with the sound of his language—never his elaborate mythological systems. I know I learned two things from his poetry, and those two things were at war with each other. One was that poetry can be "about," can root itself in, politics. Even if it is a defense of privilege, even if it deplores political rebellion and revolution, it can, may have to, account for itself politically, consciously situate itself amid political conditions, without sacrificing intensity of language. The other, that politics leads to "bitterness" and "abstractness" of mind, makes women shrill and hysterical, and is finally a waste of beauty and talent: "Too long a sacrifice / can make a stone of the heart." There was absolutely nothing in the literary canon I knew to counter the second idea. Elizabeth Barrett Browning's anti-slavery and feminist poetry, H.D.'s anti-war and woman-identified poetry, like the radical— yes, revolutionary—work of Langston Hughes and Muriel Rukeyser, were still buried by the academic literary canon. But the first idea was extremely important to me: a poet—one who was apparently certified—could actually write about political themes, could weave the names of political activists into a poem:

MacDonagh and MacBride
And Connally and Pearce
Now and in time to come
Wherever green is worn
Are changed, changed utterly:
A terrible beauty is born.

As we all do when young and searching for what we can't even name yet, I took what I could use where I could find it. When the ideas or forms we need are banished, we seek their residues wherever we can trace them. But there was one major problem with this. I had been born a woman, and I was trying to think and act as if poetry—and the possibility of making poems—were a universal—a gender-neutral—realm. In the universe of the masculine paradigm, I naturally absorbed ideas about women, sexuality, power from the subjectivity of male poets—Yeats not the least among them. The dissonance between these images and the daily events of my own life demanded a constant footwork of imagination, a kind of perpetual translation, and an unconscious fragmentation of identity: woman from poet. Every group that lives under the naming and image-making power of a dominant culture is at risk from this mental fragmentation and needs an art which can resist it.

Joy Harjo answered the 500th anniversary of the Columbus invasion with her spirit-soaring poetry reading on October 13, 1992.
(artwork by Hal BrightCloud)

from *Writing With The Sun*   Joy Harjo

On my eighth birthday I was given a Louis Untermeyer collection of poetry for children. I was surprised my mother had read my secret desire for books of poetry. We had no books in our home except for a Bible my mother gave me when I began attending church for the singing and storytelling. Later, I brought home books from the library. My mother had an eighth grade education from a one-room school in northwestern Arkansas. Eighth grade was all that could be afforded in clothes and shoes for her and for the six boys in the family. The children were needed for labor; books were a luxury. The only book she had in her home was a family Bible which was used as a repository of information on births and deaths, not for poetry or stories.

My mother quoted a William Blake poem once from memory, a poem she'd been forced to memorize at school. From her recitation I understood that the poem was foreign to her, from a place and time that excluded her. But then her memories of school were painful. She was teased for her ragged clothes, her lard pail lunches of biscuits, lard and water gravy. Education meant fist fights and embarrassment. Yet, I understood that she loved poetry. This was poetry, this stuff of sound and grace. But it was her singing to the radio that made me understand her love of poetry. I listened more closely then to the rattling whistle of the world. I made my own songs in the dark. When she gave me the gift of a book of poetry she must have recognized that particular hunger burning me, for it lit her heart as she wrote songs long after the children were asleep.

It's at this age I associate poetry with books, with words printed precisely on the page in perfect rows. I've forgotten talking to the sun. I am a prodigious reader and prolific artist, yet the words appear to belong to someone else. I stumble over them, duck, and avoid confrontation. My identity is eaten up by fear. I don't know where to place myself in these classes of students who are predominantly white. There are a few Indian students here and there. We are the largest minority, but we don't wish to call attention to ourselves. I don't know how to speak. It becomes a problem. Notes are sent home to my parents. Maybe I don't give them the notes, or they don't have time to respond, or my mother is too intimidated to deal with school officials. My parents divorce and my mother works two and sometimes three jobs. I eventually handle all school correspondence for my brothers and sister and myself. Poetry belongs to someone else. It's a tradition that belongs to the other children.

One poem stands out from the struggle of those times. Emily Dickinson spoke to me from winged pages: "I'm nobody, who are you? / Are you nobody, too?" Her voice penetrated the soft wet earth of the bog beneath the

wordlessness, loosened the fertile underground in the place of great losses.
Poetry was revealed as a sacred language, something I didn't find in the
church and Sunday school I attended alone and then with my sister. It was a
gift from a woman who searched out her own truth in the judgmental Puritan
enclave of this country. The images called sacred were constructed for her by
the fathers and the church. She was no place to be found in those unrelenting
places, but there in her room where the sun came in to speak those rare
mornings she met herself and the poetry that became her.

Yet the distilled and potent image of poetry from the sum total of my
education—from the Tulsa public schools, church and Indian boarding school—
an image that followed me into the university when I decided to become first
a surgeon, a painter, and then a poet was this: a man in a tweed coat with a
gray beard on a face pale from little sun recites obscure verses in an institute
of stern brick. He is unapproachable. His poems have nothing to do with the
intricate images of my life as a Muscogee woman from Oklahoma, of a people
who were exiled from their homelands by people who spoke his language.

When I came to poetry it was through the struggles of tribal peoples to
assert our human rights, to secure our sovereign rights as nations in the early
seventies. It was the struggle begun by my grandmothers and grandfathers
when they fought the move from our homelands in the Southeast to Indian
Territory. This, too, was my personal struggle as a poet. It was in this wave of
cultural renaissance for Indian peoples in this country that I heard the poetry
that would change me, a poetry that could have been written those mornings
of creation from childhood. This poetry named me as it jolted the country into
sharp consciousness.

I heard the poetry of Simon Ortiz, an Acoma Pueblo poet who wrote of the
sacred in the everyday; the poetry of Leslie Silko from Laguna Pueblo, whose
stunning images still run through my bloodstream; of Scott Momaday, from
the Kiowa people, who was in love with words and the land that made them.
Their poetry of this land, a land that mothers all those who step out onto the
earth from between their mothers' legs. The land that fed each of us, clothed
us, blessed us.

Poetry for the People Guest Poets Answer Questions About the Canon, featuring Cornelius Eady, Marilyn Chin, Ntozake Shange, Dan Bellm, Alfred Arteaga and Janice Gould

Poetry for the People: What are your thoughts on the canon, its usefulness and uselessness?

Cornelius Eady: As an African-American poet who also makes his living within the academy, the question of whether or not there should be a canon tugs at both parts of my personality, the academic who has come to appreciate the various stories we tell in order to say who we are as a culture, and the poet who knows what has been in most cases ignored, devalued or purposely left out.

After writing and teaching literature for most of my adult life, I can make at least two personal observations: one, that for me, literature is a living breathing tradition, in which the past is forever informing the present; two: the main reason for literature is to answer the basic human question "Who am I?" If I am Shakespeare, then I am Griot; if I am Homer, then I am Li Po; if I am Melville, then I am Phillis Wheatley.

If there is a "truth" about our culture, it may be the fact that the story of who we all are is much, much more than the narrow definitions most of us who teach today were forced to encounter when we first entered college. A truly useful and necessary canon will welcome and acknowledge that simple but thorny reality.

Marilyn Chin: My personal psychology regarding "the canon" is this: To the outer world I say in a devil-may-care manner "to hell with it." It's a fixed endgame: There will always be an imperialist, Eurocentric bias. The powers-that-be who lord over the selection process are and forevermore will be privileged white male critics. They will decide who will be validated along with Shakespeare and Milton and the latter-day saints of the like of Keats, Yeats and Eliot. They will guard that "canon" jealously with their elaborate "critical" apparatus; and driven by their own Darwinian instinct to "survive" they will do the best they can to "exclude" us and to promote their own monolithic vision.

But deep inside me another voice rings resolute. I am a serious poet with a rich palette and important missive and I shall fight for the survival of my poetry. What I learned from my youth as a marginalized and isolated west coast Asian American poet is this: it's no fun to be "excluded"…as a matter of fact, it feels like hell. What is the purpose of spending most of your adult life hunched in a dark corner perfecting your poems, if your ouvre will be buried and forgotten anyway? I don't believe any poet who tells me, "No, baby, I don't give a damn about the canon." I am certain that the very same poet has his little poems all dressed up, organized and alphabetized and locked in a vault to be opened in the next century.

The poet's mission on earth is to inspire and to illuminate; and to leave behind to our glorious descendents an intricate and varied map of humanity. One way to survive is to be like Milton, who sits aloft in the great pantheon in the sky and only a very few self-flagellating geeky scholar/poets could indulge into his knotty points. Another way to survive is to be like Gwendolyn Brooks; I predict that her poem "We Real Cool" will be warm on school children's lips forever. To survive is to be like Langston Hughes, whose poem "A Raisin in the Sun" inspired the young playwright Lorraine Hansberry to write a masterpiece bearing that same name. The true test of "validation" is when one's poems can serve as inspirational models and guiding spirits for a younger generation. We must survive! We must fight to be included in "the canon," so that our voices will sing through history and the global consciousness in eternal echoes. And I'll be damned if I'm going to miss out on THAT out-of-the-body experience!

Poetry for the People: Which poems/poets have been most relevant to you? How did certain poets influence you when you first started writing poetry? What did you try to emulate?

Ntozake Shange: Le Roi Jones' *Preface to a Twenty-Volume Suicide Note* (1962) let me know that words change shape, and history (ours) is present and prescient in the most personal avenues.

Dan Bellm: Poetry in Spanish—especially Pablo Neruda, Manlio Argueta, Miguel Hernández, Ernesto Cardenal. Trying to get that kind of music into English—and trying my hand at translation. When I began to write poetry seriously (in my 30s) I turned most to a couple of American poets—Elizabeth Bishop and James Schuyler for their simplicity of language and their attention to *seeing* the world as it is (also Robert Hass and Brenda Hillman).

Alfred Arteaga: My multilingual writing was inspired by Alurista. When I came upon "Nationchild Plumaroja" in 1972 I was thoroughly shaken by the possibilites. The Mexican poet, Jaime Ruiz Reyes, also proved significant for me. Finally, Sor Juana Ines de la Cruz, the 17th-century Mexican writer, constantly inspires and intimidates: work so brilliant, so intense.

Poetry for the People: In your opinion, what poet(s) and poem(s) especially demonstrate an individual manner of writing poetry while also claiming or transforming a cultural identity?

Ntozake Shange: Leon Damas, Le Roi Jones, Susan Griffin, Judy Grahn, Carolyn Rodgers, Jessica Hagedorn, Pedro Pietri, Adrienne Rich, Carolyn Forché, and June Jordan, of course.

Janice Gould: Many of the writers whose work I'm familiar with claim a cultural identity, but at the same time they are aware of the many identities we negotiate as we strategize our survival and continuance in U.S. society.

I don't know anyone who writes like Joy Harjo or like Chrystos. Both of these women identify as American Indian in their work. This identity, and its permutations of meaning, are present and powerful in their work. It informs their consciousness….

Sandra Cisneros, a Mexican American writer from the Midwest, also blazes with wonderful richness and intensity. She's liable to say any wicked thing, to call another woman a "goofy white woman" when she's feeling bitchy, or tell her lover "you bring out the colonizer in me./ The holocaust of desire in me." She's exuberant and runs the risk of appearing to be a hot chili queen, but she negotiates this stereotype adroitly, humorously. She uses it, stands it on its head with the turn of a phrase, saying something luscious and unforgettable.

Alfred Arteaga: In general, Chicano poets seem to undertake matters of subject identity and cross these with matters of language. The intercultural subject gets played out in the interlingual lines. This is perhaps the most significant feature of Chicano poetry. Alurista, Lorna Dee Cervantes, Juan Felipe Herrera, Cherrie Moraga all do this.

Leroy Quintana: Sherman Alexie comes to mind. You learn the pain of reservation life, but he never preaches. Leo Romero, a fellow New Mexican portrays that culture well. I like Martin Espada's work because it teaches me a lot about Puerto Rican life. Juan Felipe Herrera does a lot of interesting surrealist stuff, as does Victor Martinez, who should have a lot more recognition for his book *Looking For a House*. Richard Garcia, author of *The Flying Garcias*, is a great writer. And Timothy Liu is very clear, but very complex—makes poetry seem easy. I recommend his *Vox Angelica*.

Dan Bellm: Adrienne Rich and Allen Ginsberg especially come to mind: daring queer poets—like their/our ancestors, Walt Whitman and Emily Dickinson.

Poetry for the People: What advice would you give to poets just beginning to acquaint themselves with new poetry from noncanonical literary or cultural traditions?

Leroy Quintana: There's no remedy but hard work. You have to explore, make yourself available to every poem/tradition so that every poem can make itself available to you. Because a lot of this is not mainstream stuff—you need to find catalogs and order it. You need to haunt bookstores and make discoveries.

Dan Bellm: Read and listen widely; suspend judgements that are based on what "mainstream" publishers and critics define as worthy; get away from the printed page, and out of the house; go to poetry readings; seek out poets who come from worlds/cultures/language traditions other than your own.

Janice Gould: If you like poetry, read it, read it a lot. Think about it, analyze it. Talk about it with your friends, your teachers, other poets. Try to understand it and what it is teaching you. And if you like to write poetry, write it. Be brave and share it with others. Ask for critique. I like to think we should all try to be unprejudiced in our tastes, to sample as much as we can from as wide a range as we can…. Give poetry your undying support.

Poetry for the People: Is there anything else about poetry you want to add?

Ntozake Shange: I use poetry the way some people use encyclopedias: to find out more. I listen for a voice that springs from a real breath, a sweating body that speaks, or I stop reading.

CREATING OUR OWN CANON: IN-YOUR-FACE AMERICA BIBLIOGRAPHIES

Drawing on reading lists and recommendations from guest poets, rap sessions, disagreements, and revelations, we have compiled a beginning bibliography of poets from several different traditions. We say "beginning bibliography" because these lists do not presume to create a new Final List of Everything the Well-Versed Poet Should Know. Many of the works can be cross-listed under different categories. We hope you will create your own categories and lists, adding the new poets published in the last chapter of this book, the elementary school poets featured in the outreach chapter, and all of the people whom *you* know personally, publishing in chapbooks or 'zines, reading aloud in classes and cafés and living rooms and libraries.

Tara Clay, Golden Brooks, and James Joyner creating new American poetry. (photo by Samiya Bashir and Ananda Esteva)

African American Poetry

recommended by Professor June Jordan

Baraka, Imamu Amiri. *The Dead Lecturer*. New York: Grove Press, 1964.
———. *Preface To a Twenty-Volume Suicide Note*. New York: Totem Press in association with Corinth Books, 1961.
———. *Selected Poetry of Amiri Baraka/LeRoi Jones*. 1st ed. New York: Morrow, 1979.

Brooks, Gwendolyn. *Selected Poems*. 1st ed. New York: Harper & Row, 1963.
———. *The Near-Johannesburg Boy and Other Poems*. Chicago: Third World Press, 1991.

Brown, Sterling Allen. *The Collected Poems of Sterling A. Brown*. Selected by Michael S. Harper. 1st ed. New York: Harper & Row, 1980.

Datcher, Michael, ed. *My Brothers Keeper: Blackmen's Poetry Anthology*. Berkeley, CA: M. Datcher, 1992.

Davis, Thulani. *Playing the Changes*. 1st ed. Middletown, CT: Wesleyan University Press, 1985.

Eady, Cornelius. *The Gathering of My Name*. Pittsburgh: Carnegie Mellon University Press, 1991.
———. *Kartunes*. West Orange, NJ: Warthog Press, 1980.
———. *Victims of the Latest Dance Craze*. 1st ed. Chicago: Ommation Press, 1985.
———. *You Don't Miss Your Water*. New York: Henry Holt, 1995.

Forman, Ruth. *We Are the Young Magicians*. Boston: Beacon Press, 1993.

Hayden, Robert Earl. *Collected Poems*. Edited by Frederick Glaysher. 1st ed. New York: Liveright, 1985.

Jordan, June. *Haruko: Love Poems*. 1st U.S. ed. New York: High Risk Books, 1994.
———. *Naming Our Destiny: New And Selected Poems*. New York: Thunder's Mouth Press, 1989.
———. *I was Looking at the Ceiling and then I Saw the Sky*. New York: Scribner, 1995.

Knight, Etheridge. *Belly Song and Other Poems*. 1st ed. Detroit: Broadside Press, 1973.

Komunyakaa, Yusef. *Neon Vernacular: New and Selected Poems*. Middletown, CT: Wesleyan University Press; Hanover, NH: University Press of New England, 1993.

Lorde, Audre. *Chosen Poems, Old And New*. New York: W.W. Norton and Co., 1982.

Madhubuti, Haki R. *Don't Cry, Scream*. Introduction by Gwendolyn
Brooks. 25th year anniversary ed. Chicago: Third World Press, 1992.

Miller, E. Ethelbert, ed. *In Search of Color Everywhere: A Collection of
African-American Poetry*. New York: Stewart, Tabori and Chang, 1994.

———. *First Light: New and Selected Poems*. Baltimore, MD: Black Classic
Press, 1994.

Patterson, Raymond R. *26 Ways of Looking at a Black Man and Other
Poems*. New York: Award Books, 1969.

Peters, Erskine. *Lyrics of the Afro-American Spiritual: A Documentary
Collection*. Westport, CT: Greenwood Press, 1993.

Sanchez, Sonia. *Under a Soprano Sky*. Trenton, NJ: Africa World Press, 1987.

Shange, Ntozake. *A Daughter's Geography*. New York: St. Martin's Press,
1983.

———. *For colored girls who have considered suicide, when the rainbow
is enuf: a choreopoem*. New York: Collier Books, 1989.

Sundiata, Sekou. *Freeo*. New York: Shamal Books, 1977.

Troupe, Quincy. *Snake-Back Solos: Selected Poems, 1969–1977*. New York:
I. Reed Books, 1978.

Williams, Sherley Anne. *Some One Sweet Angel Chile*. New York: William
Morrow and Co., 1982.

———. *Working Cotton*. San Diego, CA: Harcourt, Brace, Jovanovich, 1992.

Different attitudes and
somebody's knee.
(photo by June Jordan)

Asian American Poetry

recommended by Marilyn Chin, Dorothy Wang, and others

Ai. *Cruelty; Killing Floor: Poems*. New York: Thunder's Mouth Press, 1987.

Chin, Marilyn. *Dwarf Bamboo*. Greenfield Center: Greenfield Review Press, 1987.

———. *The Phoenix Gone, The Terrace Empty*. Minneapolis: Milkweed Editions, 1994.

Hahn, Kimiko. *Earshot*. 1st ed. Brooklyn: Hanging Loose Press, 1992.

———. *Air Pocket*. Brooklyn: Hanging Loose Press, 1989.

Hongo, Garrett Kaoru. *The Buddha Bandits Down Highway 99: Poetry*. Mountain View: Buddhahead Press, 1978.

———. *Yellow Light*. 1st ed. Middletown, CT: Wesleyan University Press, 1982.

Inada, Lawson Fusao. *Before The War: Poems As They Happened*. New York: William Morrow and Co., 1971.

Lee, Li-Young. *The City In Which I Love You: Poems*. 1st ed. Brockport, NY: BOA Editions, 1990.

———. *The Winged Seed: A Remembrance*. New York: Simon and Schuster, 1995.

Mirikitani, Janice. *Shedding Silence*. Berkeley, CA: Celestial Arts, 1987.

Mura, David. *After We Lost Our Way*. New York: E.P. Dutton, 1989.

Shiraishi, Kazuko. *Seasons of Sacred Lust: The Selected Poems of Kazuko Shiraishi*. Edited and with an Introduction by Kenneth Rexroth. Translated by Ikuko Atsumi et al. New York: New Directions Publishing Corp., 1978.

Sze, Arthur. *Dazzled: Poems*. Point Reyes Station, CA: Floating Island Publications, 1982.

———. *River River*. Providence, RI: Lost Roads Publishers, 1987.

Tsui, Kitty. *The Words of a Woman Who Breathes Fire*. 1st ed. San Francisco, CA: Spinsters Ink, 1983.

The Women of South Asian Descent Collective, eds. *Our Feet Walk the Sky: Women of the South Asian Diaspora*. San Francisco: Aunt Lute Books, 1993.

Wong, Nellie. *Dreams in Harrison Railroad Park: Poems*. Berkeley, CA: Kelsey St. Press, 1977.

Yamada, Mitsuye. *Camp Notes and Other Poems*. San Lorenzo, CA: Shameless Hussy Press, 1976.

Asian American Anthologies

Bruchac, Joseph, ed. *Breaking Silence: An Anthology of Contemporary Asian American Poets*. 1st ed. Greenfield Center, NY: Greenfield Review Press, 1983.

Chan, Jeffery Paul, ed. *The Big Aiiieeeee!: An Anthology of Chinese American and Japanese American Literature*. New York: Meridan, 1991.

Chiang, Fay. *In the City of Contradictions*. 1st ed. New York: Sunbury Press, 1979.

Hongo, Garrett, ed. *The Open Boat: Poems from Asian America*. 1st ed. New York: Anchor Books, 1993.

Komachi, Ono No and Izumi Shikibu. *The Ink Dark Moon: Love Poems*. Translated by Jane Hirshfield and Mariko Aratani. 1st ed. New York: Vintage Books, 1990.

Kono, Juliet S. and Cathy Song, ed. *Sister Stew: Fiction and Poetry by Women*. Honolulu, HI: Bamboo Ridge Press, 1991.

Lowitz, M. Leza, Aoyama Miyuka, and Akemi Tomioka, eds. and trans. *A Long Rainy Season: Haiku and Tanka*. Berkeley, CA: Stone Bridge Press, 1994.

Mirikitani, Janice, ed. *Time to Greez!: Incantations from the Third World*. Third World Communications. San Francisco: Glide Publications, 1975.

Wang, L. Ling-Chi and Henry Yiheng Zhao, eds. *Chinese American Poetry: An Anthology*. Seattle: University of Washington Press, 1991.

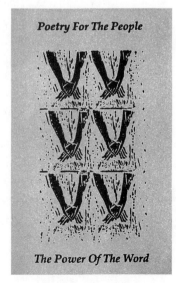

Cover from the Poetry for the People Anthology **The Power of the Word**. (Artwork by Elizabeth Meyer)

Caribbean Poetry

recommended by Professor VéVé Clark

These titles cover the Caribbean area in four language categories: Creole, English, French, and Spanish. The selection includes anthologies and studies that are available in the United States and Jamaica. For more recent single volumes of poetry published in the Caribbean or Britain, consult the Berry anthology (1984) or Chamberlin's bibliography (1993).

Arnold, A. James. *Modernism and Negritude: The Poetry and Poetics of Aimé Cesaire*. Cambridge, MA: Harvard University Press, 1981.

Bennett, Louise. *Selected Poems*. Kingston, Jamaica: Sangster's Book Stores, 1982.

Berry, James, ed. *News for Babylon: The Chatto Book of West Indian-British Poetry*. London: Chatto & Windus, 1984.

Brathwaite, Kamau. *Islands*. Oxford and New York: Oxford University Press, 1969.

———. *Third World Poems*. Harlow, Essex, England: Longman, 1983.

———. *Masks*. Oxford and New York: Oxford University Press, 1968.

Cesaire, Aimé. *Aimé Cesaire: The Collected Poetry*. Translated and with an Introduction by Clayton Eshleman and Annette Smith. Berkeley: University of California Press, 1983.

Figueroa, John, ed. *Caribbean Voices: An Anthology of West Indian Poetry*. London: Evans Bros., 1971.

Guillèn, Nicolas. *Patria o Muerte! The Great Zoo, and Other Poems*. Translated and edited by Robert Marquez. New York: Monthly Review Press, 1972.

Mordecai, Pamela, ed. *From Our Yard: Jamaican Poetry Since Independence*. Kingston, Jamaica: Institute of Jamaica Publications, 1987.

Morejon, Nancy. *Where the Island Sleeps Like a Wing: Selected Poetry*. Translated by Kathleen Weaver. San Francisco: Black Scholar Press, Distributed for Ediciones Vitral, 1985.

Rosenbaum, Sidonia Carmen. *Modern Women Poets of Spanish America: The Precursors, Delmira Agustini, Gabriela Mistral, Alfonsina Storni, Juana de Ibarbourou*. Westport, CT: Greenwood Press, 1978.

Chicana/o, Latina/o American Poetry

recommended by Professor Alfred Arteaga and others

Alarcon, Francisco X. *Body In Flames (Cuerpo En Llamas)*. Translated by Francisco Aragon. San Francisco: Chronicle Books, 1990.

Alurista. *Floricanto en Aztlán*. Los Angeles: Chicano Cultural Center, University of California, 1971.

———. *Nationchild plumaroja*. San Diego: Toltecas en Aztlán Centro Cultural de la Raza, 1972.

Anzaldúa, Gloria. *Borderlands: The New Mestiza (La frontera)*. San Francisco: Spinsters/Aunt Lute, 1987.

Arteaga, Alfred. *Cantos*. Berkeley, CA: Chusma House Publications, 1991.

Baca, Jimmy Santiago. *Black Mesa Poems*. New York: New Directions Publishing Corp., 1989.

Castillo, Ana. *My Father was a Toltec and Selected Poems, 1973–1988*. 1st ed. New York: Norton, 1995.

———. *Women are not Roses*. Houston, TX: Arte Publico Press, 1984.

Cervantes, Lorna Dee. *From the Cables of Genocide: Poems On Love And Hunger*. Houston, TX: Arte Publico Press, 1991.

———. *Emplumada*. Pittsburgh, PA: University of Pittsburgh Press, 1981.

Cisneros, Sandra. *My Wicked, Wicked Ways*. Berkeley, CA: Third Woman Press, 1987.

Corpi, Lucha. *Variations On A Storm (Variaciones Sobre Una Tempestad)*. Translated by Catherine Rodriguez-Nieto. Berkeley, CA: Third Woman Press, 1990.

Gonzales, Rodolfo. *I am Joaquin*. Santa Barbara, CA: La Causa Publications, 1967.

Herrera, Juan Felipe. *Exiles Of Desire*. Houston, TX: Arte Publico Press, 1985.

Moraga, Cherrié. *Loving In The War Years: Lo Que Nunca Paso Por Sus Labios*. Boston, MA: South End Press, 1983.

Quintana, Leroy. *Sangre*. Las Cruces, NM: Prima Agua Press, 1981.

———. *Five Poets of Aztlán*. Tempe, AZ: Bilingual Press, 1984.

———. *The History of Home*. Tempe, AZ: Bilingual Press, 1993.

Rodriguez, Luis J. *The Concrete River*. 1st ed. Willimantic, CT: Curbstone Press, 1991.

Sánchez, Ricardo. *Canto y Grito mi Liberacíon….* El Paso, TX: Mictla Publications, 1971.

Soto, Gary. *The Elements of San Joaquin*. Pittsburgh: University of Pittsburgh Press, 1977.

Children's Poetry

recommended by June Jordan, Pamela Wilson, and others

Adoff, Arnold. *Black Out Loud: An Anthology of Modern Poems by Black Americans*. New York: Macmillan, 1970.

———. *I Am the Darker Brother: An Anthology of Modern Poems by Black Americans*. New York: Collier Books, 1970.

Baron, Virginia Olsen. *Here I Am: An Anthology of Poems Written by Young People in Some of America's Minority Groups*. 1st ed. New York: Dutton, 1969.

Brooks, Gwendolyn. *Bronzeville Boys and Girls*. New York: Harper, 1956.

Jordan, June. "The Voice of the Children" from *Civil Wars*. Boston: Beacon Press, 1981.

Jordan, June, ed. *Soulscript: Afro-American Poetry*. New York: Zenith Books, Doubleday and Company, 1970.

Jordan, June and Terri Bush. *The Voice of the Children*. New York: Holt, Rinehart and Winston, Inc., 1970.

Koch, Kenneth. *Wishes, Lies and Dreams; Teaching Children to Write Poetry*. New York: Chelsea House Publishers, 1970.

Kohl, Herbert. *36 Children*. New York: The New American Library, 1967.

Lopate, Phillip. *Being With Children: A High Spirited Personal Account of Teaching Writing, Theatre and Videotape*. New York: Doubleday and Company, Inc., 1975.

Lotu, Denize. *Father and Son*. New York: Philomel Books, 1992.

Myers, Walter Dean. *Brown Angels: An Album of Pictures and Verse*. 1st ed. New York: HarperCollins, 1993.

Soto, Gary. *Neighborhood Odes*. San Diego: Harcourt Brace Jovanovich, 1992.

———. *A Fire in My Hands: A Book of Poems*. New York: Scholastic, 1990.

Sullivan, Charles, ed. *Children of Promise: African-American Literature and Art for Young People*. New York: Harry N. Abrams, 1991.

Children's Poetry Anthologies

Brandenberg, Franz, et al. *Home: A Collaboration of Thirty Distinguished Authors and Illustrators of Children's Books to Aid the Homeless*. Edited by Michael J. Rosen. 1st ed. New York: HarperCollins, 1992.

Janeczko, Paul B., ed. *The Music of What Happens: Poems That Tell Stories*. New York: Orchard Books, 1988.

Morrison, Lillian, ed. *Rhythm Road: Poems to Move to.* 1st ed. New York: Lothrop, Lee & Shepard Books, 1988.

Rubadiri, David, ed. *Growing Up with Poetry: An Anthology for Secondary Schools.* Oxford: Heinemann International, 1989.

Shihab Nye, Naomi, ed. *This Same Sky: A Collection of Poems from Around the World.* 1st ed. New York: Four Winds Press, 1992.

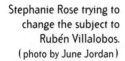 

Stephanie Rose trying to change the subject to Rubén Villalobos.
(photo by June Jordan)

Resources on Deaf Poetry

recommended by Ella Mae Lentz

Fourteen Types of Rhyme   Shelly Teves

When I suggested that we invite a deaf poet into our class as a guest lecturer,
I discovered a disturbing lack of enthusiasm. Nevertheless, I arranged for Ella
Mae Lentz to visit our class. Ella teaches American Sign Language (ASL) at
Vista College in downtown Berkeley. In her forty-five minute lecture, she
discussed the history of deaf culture and ASL, demonstrated the difference
between ASL and signing English, touched on some technical aspects of ASL
poetry and performed several of her own poems. I was amazed to learn that
there are fourteen different ways to rhyme in ASL, but in English, only three. I
was also thrilled by the class's response to Ella. Everyone loved her. After class,
one student teacher poet even said that he had learned more from Ella's
lecture than from any of the others.

A Note on Deaf Poetry   Professor Jennifer Nelson

Deaf poetry is not textual in the traditional sense: Deaf poetry is a sign
language poetry, a bodily one, and is performed for an audience or videotape.
Although Deaf textual poetry exists, it is just poetry in the usual, hearing sense,
and isn't seen by some members of the Deaf culture as Deaf poetry. American
Sign Language poets include Clayton Valli, Peter Cook, and Ella Mae Lentz. In
Motion Press, SignMedia and Sign Enhancers distribute ASL poetry tapes. There
is also a relatively large collection of American Sign Language poetry tapes at
the Gallaudet University library in Washington, DC.

Adler, Frances Payne. *Raising the Tents*. Corvallis, OR: Calyx Books, 1993.
Bankier, Joanna, ed. *The Other Voice: Twentieth-Century Women's Poetry
    in Translation*. Foreword by Adrienne Rich. 1st ed. New York: W.W.
    Norton and Co., 1976.
Lucus, Ceil and Clayton Valli. *Language Contact in the American Deaf
    Community*. San Diego: Academic Press, 1992.
Valli, Clayton. *Linguistics of American Sign Language: A Resource Text for
    ASL*. Washington, DC: Gallaudet University Press, 1992.
Van Cleve, John V., ed. *Gallaudet Encyclopedia of Deaf People and Deafness*.
    New York: McGraw-Hill, 1987.

Gay and Lesbian Poetry

recommended by Dan Bellm

Beck, Evelyn Torton, ed. *Nice Jewish Girls: A Lesbian Anthology.* Watertown, MA: Persephone Press, 1982.

Bellm, Dan. *A Story in a Bottle.* San Francisco: Norton Coker Press, 1991.

Bulkin, Elly and Joan Larkin, eds. *Lesbian Poetry: An Anthology.* Watertown, MA: Persephone Press, 1981.

Coote, Stephen, ed. *Penguin Book of Homosexual Verse.* NY: Penguin, 1983.

Grahn, Judy. *The Work of a Common Woman: The Collected Poetry of Judy Grahn, 1964–1977.* New York: St. Martin's Press, 1980.

Hemphill, Essex, ed. *Brother to Brother: New Writings by Black Gay Men.* 1st ed. Boston: Alyson Publications, 1991.

Hunter, B. Michael, ed. *Sojourner: Black Gay Voices in the Age of AIDS.* New York: Other Countries Press, 1993.

Leyland, Winston, ed. *Angels of the Lyre: A Gay Poetry Anthology.* San Francisco: Panjandrum Press, 1975.

———. *Orgasms of Light: The Gay Sunshine Anthology, Poetry, Short Fiction, Graphics.* San Francisco: Gay Sunshine Press, 1977.

Moraga, Cherríe and Gloria Anzaldúa, eds. *This Bridge Called My Back: Writings by Radical Women of Color.* Watertown, MA: Persephone Press, 1981.

Morse, Carl and Joan Larkin, eds. *Gay & Lesbian Poetry in Our Time: An Anthology.* 1st ed. New York: St. Martin's Press, 1988.

Pratt, Minnie Bruce. *Crime Against Nature.* Ithaca, NY: Firebrand Books, 1990.

Ramos, Juanita, ed. *Compañeras: Latina Lesbians: An Anthology.* 1st ed. New York: Routledge, 1987.

Roscoe, Will, ed. *Living the Spirit: A Gay American Indian Anthology.* New York: St. Martin's Press, 1988.

Saint, Assoto, ed. *The Road Before Us: 100 Gay Black Poets.* New York: Galiens Press, 1991.

Silvera, Makeda, ed. *Piece of My Heart: A Lesbian of Color Anthology.* Toronto: Sister Vision, 1991.

Smith, Barbara, ed. *Home Girls: A Black Feminist Anthology.* New York: Kitchen Table/Women of Color Press, 1983.

Young, Ian, ed. *The Male Muse: A Gay Anthology.* Trumansburg, NY: The Crossing Press, 1973.

———. *The Son of the Male Muse: New Gay Poetry.* Trumansburg, NY: The Crossing Press, 1983.

More Indispensable Lesbian and Gay American Poets

Francisco X. Alarcon, Dorothy Allison, John Ashbery, James Baldwin, Frank Bidart, Elizabeth Bishop, James Broughton, Olga Broumas, Cheryl Clarke, Emily Dickinson, Tim Dlugos, Mark Doty, Robert Duncan, Edward Field, Amy Gerstler, Allen Ginsberg, Susan Griffin, Thom Gunn, Marylin Hacker, Eloise Klein Healy, Essex Hemphill, Richard Howard, Langston Hughes, Rudy Kikel, Wayne Koestenbaum, Joan Larkin, Audre Lorde, James Merrill, Paul Monette, Honor Moore, Cherrié Moraga, Eileen Myles, Harold Norse, Frank O'Hara, Mary Oliver, Pat Parker, Adrienne Rich, Muriel Rukeyeser, James Schuyler, Gertrude Stein, May Swenson, David Trinidad, and Walt Whitman.

Gay and Lesbian Journals

Calyx, *Common Lives/Lesbian Lives*, *Conditions*, *The Evergreen Chronicles*, *Hanging Loose*, *Heresies*, *IKON*, *Other Countries*, *RFD*, *Sinister Wisdom*, *13th Moon*, *The James White Review*.

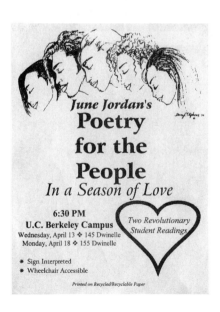

A flyer announcing student readings of **Poetry in a Season of Love**.
(artwork by Darryl Stephens)

Irish and Irish American Poetry

recommended by Professor David Lloyd and others

Boland, Eavan. *The Journey*. Dublin: Gallery Press, 1983.

Carson, Ciaran. *Belfast Confetti*. Winston-Salem, NC: Wake Forest University Press, 1989.

———. *First Language: Poems*. Winston-Salem, NC: Wake Forest University Press, 1994.

Joyce, Trevor. *Pentahedron*. Dublin: New Writers' Press, 1972.

Kinsella, Thomas. *New Poems and Selected Poems,1973*. Dublin: Dolmen Press, 1973.

———. *Blood and Family*. New York: Oxford University Press, 1988.

Lloyd, David. *Change of State*. Berkeley, CA: Cusp Books, 1993.

McGuckian, Medbh. *On Ballycastle Beach*. Oxford and New York: Oxford University Press, 1988.

———. *Venus in the Rain*. New York: Oxford University Press, 1984.

Muldoon, Paul. *Meeting the British*. London and Boston: Faber and Faber, 1987.

Ni Dhomhnaill, Nuala. *Selected Poems* (Poems in Irish with English translation). Dublin: Raven Arts Press, 1986.

Paulin, Tom. *Fivemiletown*. London and Boston: Faber, 1987.

Smyth, Ailbhe, ed. *Wildish Things: An Anthology of New Irish Women's Writing*. Dublin: Attic Press, 1989.

Native American Poetry

recommended by Joy Harjo, Janice Gould, and others

Alexie, Sherman. *The Business of Fancydancing: Stories And Poems*. 1st ed. Brooklyn: Hanging Loose Press, 1992.

Allen, Paula Gunn. *Skins And Bones: Poems 1979–87*. Albuquerque, NM: West End Press, 1988.

———. *Wyrds*. San Francisco: Taurean Horn Press, 1987.

Bird, Gloria. *Full Moon on the Reservation*. 1st ed. Greenfield Center, NY: Greenfield Review Press, 1993.

Carlson, Michael. *Columbus Day: Ten Poems*. London: Northern Lights, 1984.

Chrystos. *Dream On*. Vancouver: Press Gang Publishers, 1991.

———. *In Her I Am*. Vancouver: Press Gang Publishers, 1993.

———. *Not Vanishing*. Vancouver: Press Gang Publishers, 1988.

Erdrich, Louise. *Baptism Of Desire: Poems*. 1st ed. New York: Harper & Row, 1989.

———. *Jacklight*. 1st ed. New York: Holt, Rinehart, and Winston, 1984.

Gould, Janice. *Beneath My Heart: Poetry*. Ithaca, NY: Firebrand Books, 1990.

Harjo, Joy. *In Mad Love and War*. Middletown, CN: Wesleyan University Press, 1990.

———. *Secrets from the Center of the World*. Tucson, AZ: Sun Tracks and The University of Arizona Press, 1989.

———. *She Had Some Horses*. New York: Thunder's Mouth Press, 1983.

———. *What Moon Drove Me to This?* New York, NY: I. Reed Books, 1979.

———. *The Woman Who Fell from the Sky*. New York: W.W. Norton and Co., 1994.

Hogan, Linda. *The Book of Medicines: Poems*. Minneapolis: Coffee House Press, 1993.

———. *Red Clay: Poems & Stories*. 1st ed. Greenfield Center, NY: Greenfield Review Press, 1991.

———. *Calling Myself Home*. Greenfield Center, NY: Greenfield Review Press, 1978.

Kenny, Maurice. *The Mama Poems*. Buffalo: White Pine Press, 1984.

Louis, Adrian C. *Fire Water World: Poems*. 1st ed. Albuquerque, NM: West End Press, 1989.

Naranjo-Morse, Nora. *Mud Woman: Poems From the Clay*. Tucson: University of Arizona Press, 1992.

Ortiz, Simon J. *Woven Stone.* Tucson: University of Arizona Press, 1992.

Rose, Wendy. *Bone Dance: New And Selected Poems, 1965–1993.*Tucson: University of Arizona Press, 1994.

————. *The Halfbreed Chronicles and Other Poems.* 1st ed. Albuquerque, NM: West End Press, 1985.

Stewart, Fred Mustard. *Star Child.* New York: Pocket Books, 1986.

TallMountain, Mary. *The Light On The Tent Wall: A Bridging.* Los Angeles: American Indian Studies Center, University of California, 1990.

Tapahonso, Luci. *A Breeze Swept Through.* 1st ed. Albuquerque, NM: West End Press, 1987.

————. *Sáanii Dahataat: The Women Are Singing.* Tuscon, AZ: University of Arizona Press, 1993.

Woody, Elizabeth. *Hand Into Stone: Poems.* New York: Contact II Publications, 1988.

Native American Poetry Anthologies

Brant (Degonwadonti), Beth, ed. *A Gathering of Spirit: A Collection by North American Indian Women.* Ithaca, NY: Firebrand Books, 1988.

Bruchac, Joseph, ed. *Returning the Gift: Poetry and Prose from the First North American Native Writers' Festival.* Tuscon, AZ: University of Arizona Press, 1994.

Green, Rayna, ed. *That's What She Said: Contemporary Poetry and Fiction by Native American Women.* Bloomington, IN: Indiana University Press, 1984.

Hobson, Geary, ed. *The Remembered Earth: An Anthology of Contemporary Native American Literature.* Albuquerque, NM: University of New Mexico Press, 1979.

Niatum, Duane, ed. *Harper's Anthology of 20th-Century Native American Poetry.* 1st ed. San Francisco: Harper & Row, 1988.

Rosen, Kenneth, ed. *Voices Of The Rainbow: Contemporary Poetry by Native Americans.* 1st Arcade pbk. ed. New York: Arcade Pub. (distributed by Little, Brown and Co.), 1993.

Ross, Jacob, ed. *Callaloo: A Grenada Anthology.* London: Young World Books, 1984.

Sarris, Greg, ed. *The Sound of Rattles and Clappers: A Collection of New California Indian Writing.* Tucson, AZ: University of Arizona Press, 1994.

New Women's Poetry

In addition to poetry by women in the preceding lists (especially Gwendolyn Brooks, Marilyn Chen, Thulani Davis, Ruth Forman, Janice Gould, Judy Grahn, Joy Harjo, Linda Hogan, June Jordan, Audre Lorde, Janice Mirikitani, Minnie Bruce Pratt, and Ntozake Shange), we recommend the following:

Anglesey, Zoe, ed. *IXOK AMAR GO: Central American Women's Poetry for Peace (Poesia de Mujeres Centroamericanas por la Paz)*. Penobscot, ME: Granite Press, 1987.

Brodine, Karen. *Woman Sitting at the Machine, Thinking: Poems*. 1st ed. Seattle, WA: Red Letter Press, 1990.

Collins, Martha. *A History of Small Life on a Windy Planet*. Athens: University of Georgia Press, 1993.

Heller Levi, Jan, ed. *A Muriel Rukeyser Reader*. New York: W.W. Norton and Co., 1994.

Masini, Donna. *That Kind of Danger*. Boston: Beacon Press, 1994.

Olds, Sharon. *Satan Says*. Pittsburgh: University of Pittsburgh Press, 1980.

Rich, Adrienne. *The Fact of a Doorframe: Poems Selected and New: 1950–1984*. New York: W.W. Norton and Co., 1984.

———. *An Atlas of the Difficult World: Poems, 1988–1991*. New York: W.W. Norton and Co., 1991.

———. *Diving into the Wreck: Poems 1971–1972*. 1st ed. New York: W.W. Norton and Co., 1973.

———. *What is Found There: Notebooks on Poetry and Politics*. New York: W.W. Norton and Co., 1993.

5

ALLITERATIVE SQUAT THRUSTS
A Syllabus and Some Exercises
for Writing Poetry

Poetry for the People cultivates empowerment by affirming that everybody
has something to offer—it may be up to you to define it.

—Elmirie Robinson

How a Large Dissimilar Group of Strangers
Comes Together and Shares...   Ananda Esteva

stories sweeter than honey-fried banana, old-time memories almost left to
rust, and standpoints sharp as axes, cutting down stereotypes and building us
up. The second day of class last spring, we were supposed to write our own
"How Do I Love Thee" song/poem and sing it, with Elizabeth Barrett
Browning, Queen Latifah, and Toni Braxton as our models. Now who's gonna
do that, stand up, dance up in front of a group of strangers and sing?!
Mmmmmm Hmmmm, vamos a ver! Well, up stood un hermano Mexicano, shy
dancer of El Baile Folklorico and did he sing!! He held out the fine-whine
notes of his corrido with love and dedication! One after another, more people
stood up and stripped themselves down to let us hear their deepest stories
and declarations.

A SAMPLE SYLLABUS

We hope our In-Your-Face-America bibliographies in Chapter 4 enable you to put together many different kinds of syllabi. The syllabus for our course of study changes each semester, depending on our interests and on conditions in the world that demand our attention. Some poets remain on the reading list almost every semester; these include Adrienne Rich, Ntozake Shange, Cornelius Eady, and Lorna Dee Cervantes. During the Persian Gulf War, we decided to study poets who addressed war in all its guises. We read *And Not Surrender: American Poets on Lebanon*, edited by Kanal Boullata; *Central American Women's Poetry for Peace*, edited by Zoe Anglesey; and *In Mad Love and War*, by Joy Harjo. As we attempt to discover, uncover and understand multiple poetic traditions, we compile reading lists and weave selections from them into the syllabus. The following is one sample syllabus from a semester when we were fortunate enough to have several wonderful guest lecturers who helped us to recognize the histories of different cultural traditions in poetry, and to debate and challenge the uses and limits of categories like "White" or "Native American" poetry.

Ntozake Shange dazzled the people with her exuberant, electrifying, passionate reading. (artwork by Hal BrightCloud)

Poetry For The People "In A Season of Love"

African American Studies 159 Spring '94   Prof. June Jordan

T. A. Lauren Muller

Reading List:
The Norton Anthology of Modern Poetry (2nd ed.)
Li-Young Lee, *The City in Which I Love You*
Marilyn Chin, *A Phoenix Rising: The Terrace Empty*
Cornelius Eady, *The Gathering of My Name*
Lorna Dee Cervantes, *Emplumada*
Ntozake Shange, *Nappy Edges*
Adrienne Rich, *What Is Found There*
Ciaran Carson, *The Irish For No*

Also Recommended
Thulani Davis, *Playing the Changes*
June Jordan, *Haruko/Love Poems*

Grades are based on three components:

1. *Written Component*: Over the semester students produce 10 poems, acceptable to themselves and their peers, and write a critical essay of 3–5 pages, comparing two kinds of poetry. In addition, students complete weekly writing exercises, using poems from the assigned reading as models. Their final writing folders must include exercises in the following forms, which will be introduced in lecture: sonnet, interlinear rhyme, villanelle (everyone should imitate each of these), and ballad, sestina, blues, jazz, rap (each student chooses three of these forms to imitate over the semester).

2. *Writing Workshop Component:* This includes punctual, complete, and regular attendance at class meetings, and helpful, effective critiques of other students' poetry.

3. *Publishing and Production Component*: Putting together three student readings and one anthology requires intensive work outside of class, including committee meetings, collaborative work, and participation in publicity (radio, newspaper, campus), the events themselves, and, of course, clean-up "after the party."

Poetry For The People "In A Season of Love"
African American Studies 159 Spring '94   Prof. June Jordan

Important Dates:

February 24: Poetry for the People 1991 Alumni Reading! Wheeler
Auditorium, 7:30 p.m. Reception to follow.

April 13, 18: Student Poetry Readings! 145 Dwinelle. Receptions start at
6:30 p.m., followed by readings.

Assignments, Lectures, Guest Speakers and Poets:

Jan 19:   Professor June Jordan: **Introduction to the Course** (including
Guidelines & Groundrules); discussion of sonnets by
Browning and Shakespeare; Poetry Reading by the Student
Teacher Poets.

Jan. 26:   June Jordan: **Poetic Forms: The Sonnet, The Villanelle,
Interlinear Rhyme**
Reading Assignment: Re-read Sonnet #43; "How Do I Love
Thee" by Elizabeth Barrett Browning; Sonnet #138 by
William Shakespeare and handout on the sonnet form.
Writing Assignment: 1) Write a Shakespearean or Italian sonnet
(Models: Shakespeare and Elizabeth Barrett Browning).
2) Write four lines using internal rhyme, assonance and
alliteration (Model: Percy Bysshe Shelley's "The Cloud").
3) Write three tercets using the villanelle form (Model:
Theodore Roethke, "The Waking").

Feb. 2:   June Jordan: **Oral Tradition in African American Poetry**
Reading Assignment: Adrienne Rich, *What is Found There*,
Chapter XXVI on format and form. Writing Assignment:
Write an Update of "How Do I Love Thee" and set it to music
(Models: "How Do I Love Thee," Queen Latifah; "How Do I
Love Thee," Toni Braxton; "Love's in Need of Love Today,"
The Company).

Poetry For The People "In A Season of Love"

African American Studies 159 Spring '94   Prof. June Jordan

Feb. 9:   Professor VéVé Clark: **African American and Caribbean Poetry**
Reading Assignment: Read *The Gathering of My Name* by
Cornelius Eady and *Nappy Edges* by Ntozake Shange. Note
similarities and differences. Read handout on Caribbean
Poetry, prepared by Professor VéVé Clark.
Writing Assignment: Choose a poem by Shange or Eady and
use it as a model to write your own "African American" poem.

Feb. 16:   Professor Peter Dale Scott: **"White Male" Poetry**
Reading Assignment: From the *Norton Anthology of Modern
Poetry*: Robert Frost, "Fire and Ice" and "Stopping by Woods
on a Snowy Evening"; Wallace Stevens, "Thirteen Ways of
Looking at a Blackbird" and "The Man with the Blue Guitar";
William Carlos Williams, "The Red Wheelbarrow" and "This
Is Just to Say"; T.S. Eliot, "The Love Song of J. Alfred
Prufrock"; Claude McKay, "If We Must Die"; Edna St.
Vincent Millay, "Love is Not All: It Is Not Meat nor Drink";
e.e. cummings, "my father moved through dooms of love."
Writing Assignment: Use one of these poems as a model to
write your own "White" poem.

Feb. 23:   Janice Gould: **Native American Poetry**
Reading Assignment: From the *Norton Anthology*: Louise
Erdrich, "Indian Boarding School: The Runaways" and
"Captivity"; Leslie Silko, "It Was A Long Time Before,"
"Long Time Ago," and "Toe'osh: A Laguna Coyote Story."
Begin *What Is Found There* by Adrienne Rich.
Writing Assignment: Using Silko or Erdrich as a model, write
a "Native American" poem.

Feb. 23:   **Poetry for the People: Alumni Reading**, 7:30 p.m., Wheeler
Auditorium. Featuring: Ruth Forman (*We Are the Young
Magicians*), and Michael Datcher (ed., *My Brother's Keeper*),
Hal BrightCloud, Johnson Cheu, Carina Farrero, Derrick
Gilbert, James Henry, Jamal Holmes, Margaret Lin, Claudia
May, Elizabeth Meyer, Kelly Navies, Jennie Portnof, Pamela
Stafford, Shelly Smith, and Trac Vu.

Poetry For The People "In A Season of Love"

African American Studies 159 Spring '94   Prof. June Jordan

Mar. 2:   Dan Bellm: **Gay and Lesbian Poetry**
              June Jordan: **Poetic Forms: The Blues**
              Reading Assignment: Read the packet on gay poetry prepared
              by Dan Bellm. Also read from the *Norton Anthology*: Marilyn
              Hacker, "Coda"; Audre Lorde, "Coal" and "Love Poem."
              Continue reading *What is Found There* by Adrienne Rich.
              Writing Assignment: Prepare poem for anthology submission.

Mar. 9:   Professor Charles Altieri: **The Canon**
              Reading Assignment: Packet provided by Charles Altieri:
              "Trying to Capture Rapture" and "Case In Point" by June
              Jordan; "Final Notations" and "Twenty-one Love Poems" by
              Adrienne Rich.
              Writing Assignment: Midterm Essay and Poetry Folders.

Mar. 16:   Marilyn Chin: **Asian American Poetry**
              Reading Assignment: *The Terrace Empty* and *The Phoenix
              Rising* by Marilyn Chin; *The City in Which I Love You* by
              Li-Young Lee.
              Writing Assignment: Choose a poem by Lee or Chin as a
              model for your own "Asian American" poem.

Mar. 23:   Leroy Quintana: **Chicana/o Poetry**
              Reading Assignment: Lorna Dee Cervantes, *Emplumada*
              Writing Assignment: Choose one of Cervantes' poems as a
              model for your own Chicana/o poem.

April 6:   Professor Susan Schweik: **Women's Poetry**
              Reading Assignment: Plenty of good, varied, pleasurable
              reading for Spring Break from the *Norton Anthology*:
              Muriel Rukeyser, All (pp. 880–85);
              Gwendolyn Brooks, All (pp. 973–86);
              Denise Levertov, "The Ache of Marriage" (p. 1115);
              Maxine Kumin, "In the Absence of Bliss" (pp. 1147–8),
              "Video Cuisine" (pp. 1148–49);
              Adrienne Rich, "Snapshots of a Daughter-in-Law" (pp.
              1320–23), "Face to Face" (p. 1323), "Diving into the Wreck"

Poetry For The People "In A Season of Love"

African American Studies 159 Spring '94   Prof. June Jordan

(p. 1327), from *Twenty-one Love Poems* (pp. 1329–30);
"Grandmothers" (pp. 1330–32), "Yom Kippur 1984" (pp. 1332–35);
Sylvia Plath, "Ariel" (p. 1423), "Daddy" (pp. 1424–24);
Audre Lorde, "Love Poem" (p. 1430, again), "The Women of Dan Dance with Swords in Their Hands to Mark the Time When They Were Warriors" (p. 1432);
Marge Piercy, "The Moon is Always Female" (p. 1465);
June Jordan, "Poem About My Rights" (pp. 1470–73);
Margaret Atwood, "You Fit into Me" (pp. 1545–46), "They Eat Out" (p. 1546), "Variations on the Word Love" (p. 1551);
Marilyn Hacker, from "Coda" (p. 1575, again);
Ai, All (pp. 1632–38);
Carolyn Forché, "Taking Off My Clothes" (p. 1666).
The handout, June Jordan, "Who's Rocking the Boat" (a review of women's poetry published in the March/April 1994 issue of *Ms.* Magazine.)
Writing Assignment: Choose one poem from this week's reading as a model for your own "women's" poem.

April 12:   **Rehearsal for April 13 Reading**: 3:00–6:00 p.m., 160 Dwinelle.

April 13:   Professor David Lloyd: **Irish Poetry**
              Reading Assignment: Ciaran Carson, *The Irish For No.*
              Writing Assignment: Choose one of Carson's poems as a model for your own "Irish" poem; work on poem(s) for the student reading.

April 13:   **Poetry for the People Student Reading**, 145 Dwinelle, reception starts at 6:30 p.m. Poets gather to try out mikes and go over speaking order at 6:30. People reading Monday bring food tonight for reception. All help clean up.

April 17:   **Rehearsal for April 18 Reading**: 3:00–6:00 p.m., 160 Dwinelle.

Poetry For The People "In A Season of Love"

African American Studies 159 Spring '94   Prof. June Jordan

April 18:   **Poetry for the People Student Reading**, 155 Dwinelle, reception
               starts at 6:30 p.m. Poets gather to try out mikes and go over
               order at 6:30. People reading last Wednesday, plus anyone else
               who can, bring food tonight for reception.

April 20:   Last Class! Ella Mae Lentz: **Deaf Poetry**
               Samiya Bashir and Sean Lewis: **Poetic Forms: Rap**
               Reading Assignment: Read packet prepared by Ella Mae
               Lentz.
               Writing Assignment: **Student Poetry Folders Due.**

April 25:   **Student Teacher Poetry Folders Due** by noon in June Jordan's
               box in African American Studies Office.

April 27:   **STP Folders returned** by 4:00 p.m. in boxes outside 354B
               Dwinelle.

May 3:   **Party** at Lauren's house to celebrate and distribute class
               anthology.

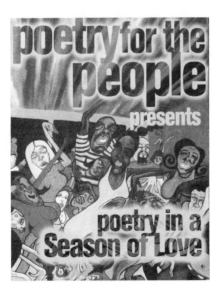

Cover from the Anthology
Poetry for the People in a
Season of Love.
(Artwork by Poetry for the
People with Sean Lewis and
Dylan Hayley)

MODELING POETIC FORMS

All poetic forms, including the villanelle, haiku, or rap, derive from particular cultural histories and traditions. Poetic structure doesn't necessarily hamper our voices. In fact, formal structure can help make our poetry clearer. When we're learning about sonnets, we're learning how to use and perhaps transform the mechanisms of control. (In other words: these little skills could help you out.)

Sonnet

Sonnets come in three general forms: Shakespearean, Italian, and irregular. All have fourteen lines and a basic rhyme and meter structure. The Shakespearean sonnet uses iambic pentameter and an *ababcdcdefefgg* rhyme scheme. The Italian sonnet also uses iambic pentameter, but has an *abbaabbacdecde* rhyme pattern. Irregular sonnets diverge from the rigid rhyme and meter structure of the Shakespearean and Italian sonnets, but maintain the fourteen-line framework.

My Middle Name   Leslie Shown

Refusing to claim a daughter gone mad
you sought the nearest child to blame
a backwards omen of the burden you had
newborn explanation of age-old pain.
Mother of my mother let me be heard
no longer a child I stand by your grave
unable to lose your poisonous words
attempting to own your bitter name.
I imagine the blows your shoulders have known
stories you were not allowed to confess
that filled every crevice where love might have grown
in a house where raised hands never fell to caress.
I come to forgive and call forgiveness Jane
to alter the meaning of family chain.

Something Like a Sonnet
for Phillis Miracle Wheatley

June Jordan

Girl from the realm of birds florid and fleet
flying full feather in far or near weather
Who fell to a dollar lust coffled like meat
Captured by avarice and hate spit together
Trembling asthmatic alone on the slave block
built by a savagery travelling by carriage
viewed like a species of flaw in the livestock
A child without safety of mother or marriage

Chosen by whimsy but born to surprise
They taught you to read but you learned how to write
Begging the universe into your eyes:
They dressed you in light but you dreamed with the night.
From Africa singing of justice and grace
your early verse sweetens the fame of our Race.

Blues

Strictly speaking, blues stanzas have three lines of verse. The first line makes a statement, the second repeats it (with or without changes), and the third resolves the stanza in a rhymed response. Of course, poets mold this structure to fit their purpose. While the strict three-lined stanza form may change, the essential repetition/call-and-response elements remain.

love blues #1   j.w. henry
(to be sung/performed)

tossed and turned last night
didn't sleep a wink
tossed and turned all night
did not sleep a wink
musta been the coffee
don't know what else to think

i might see you in the evenin'
but i'm missin' you all day
although i see you every evenin'
i'm missin' you all day
i guess i'm just a man with a
short attention span
what else can i say?

well my friends say that you' ugly
but you look so good to me
yeah all my friends say that you' ugly
but you look so good to me
difference of opinion
what else could it be?

went to write a poem
couldn't find a pen
went to write you a wide deep poem
couldn't find my favorite pen
but i've got to shine some
praise on you
if i never write again

went home turned off the t.v.
an' you know i unplugged the phone
well i turned off cable-mtv-cops
an' oprah
an' straight unplugged the phone
'cause as long as you' sittin
easy on my mind
the rest can leave me alone

they say don't try an' fight it
an' now i think i see
they say ain't no use to fight it
an' now i think i see
so i guess i'll just let it
flip turn stretch an' strut
make me close my eyes
an' signify wrap it up an' sing
sho nuff
put it in my pocket jump back an' kiss
myself an' call it love
what else can it be?

j. w. henry *was a member of the class* Poetry for the People in a Time of War *and
is published in* My Brother's Keeper, *edited by Michael Datcher.*

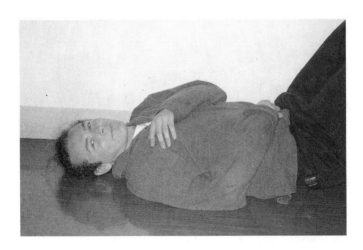

Sean Lewis rifs on Rap.
(photo by June Jordan)

Rap

The "ballad" of our days and years as we close the 21st century, rap almost always narrates a story and is meant to be delivered to a group of one's peers. The rhythmical structure is basically 4/4 (meaning four beats to a line) with as much variation and play as the poet can muster inside that frame. Extensive, rhythmical use of rhyme (end-rhyme, spicy internal rhyme, or both) is the other main characteristic of rap.

i can't believe you'd do tom cruise whose　　　　Sean Lewis

> sour sucker canary beak pucker floating yellow feather smirk
> knee-jerk gulf war t-shirt patriotism
> 　　na, na, na
> will to fuck a sheep for the frat boy jeep
> 　　　　　　hung 3 beep beep feet hi over west l.a. concrete
> 　　　　　　the supensionary disbelief that 63 impalas can't
> 　　　　　　　tip that shit
>
> 　　& dying lying down crying for the day to get skeezed
> 　　　by 72 degree venice beach pee pee
>
> 　　& dying lying-down crying by any means denying
> 　　　　　　personal responsibility
>
> katie mcgillis/jodie foster pinball machine court room scene
> 　　　　complicity
>
> 　　　　　　　denies the head on my shoulders
> 　　　　　　　　my eyes and ears
> 　　　　　　　　these knees and toes
>
> that go to sleep 8 mississippi
> 　　　　10 alligator
> 　　　　1200 frustration summer sex nuts later when
> 　　　　　fucking
>
> still stuck in the moving on up deluxe apt. on the westside elevator
> even tho i never asked edgewood properties to fix my refrigerator
>
> you damn well…
> 　　　　　they'd flake.
>
> Baby, i can't believe you'd do me too sometimes tom cruise

Rif

Never Slacken, Practice Tightness, Hope Y'all Like This   Sean Lewis

The first thing a lot of us asked when we took this class for the first time was "What's up with learning sonnets and sestinas? I thought this class was new, was different, was revolutionary!?" or, "I don't personally feel oppressed by a villanelle. Hell, if I did decide to sonnetize this rap guise, would it really help— mobilize the masses? Maybe maybe not appease the teasing degrees and self-congratulatory upper-arm squeezes of hypes, teapot mantlepiece people, and literary types eavesdropping on my classes? Is this just another version of doing just what massa' says?"

My attitude towards writing a sonnet was always that, at best, it was impractical. Maybe even dangerous. If friends started talking to you in iambic pentameter—well in a situation such as this, they might get slapped! So honoring your brother and sister poets and yourself, as a poet, and your right to predict expectations and basically knowing that really dope poets make very strong, lasting, openhanded connections, yo after having fun and handling the things that need to be done, rewriting sonnets sound pretty bunk. Upon my suggestion that he tighten up his poem, one brother poet recommended to me that I "STOP THE VIOLENCE or you be the punk." Indeed the often daunting even amusing task of separating the good stuff from the junk stunk! I never did it. Sounds a lot like torture to me. I'll make a mental note of it though, and barring armed revolution, even save that poem under the heading in my head of: "Dead Poets With No Sense of Humor, Stuff I'd Like to Do Less Than Throw a Rally in Mill Valley and Things That Make You Go Oh Hell No!" Yo, couldn't we just hook up at the reading?

This morning, I saw a graffiti tag I think sums up the whole point. Someone had written on a wall "Jesus Saves" and beneath it somebody else wrote "yo S & H Food Stamps."

DEVELOPING CULTURAL LITERACIES

One of June Jordan's Guidelines for Critiquing a Poem asks, "How does it fit into or change a tradition of poems?"

Why write White/Chicano/Native American/African American/Irish American/Asian American poetry? What are we talking about? What does African American/ Palestinian/ Korean/Jamaican mean? What is particular and distinctive about particular poetic cultural traditions in relation to a world view? What is the relationship between a particular poem and the world? How do we recognize and define existing poetic traditions without being simplistic or reductive?

In debating these questions, we rarely come to a consensus. The task of studying, responding to, and imitating various cultural traditions in poetry is both exhilirating and daunting. The following pieces were written in response to that challenge. We've included excerpts from four essays to demonstrate that analytical essays can be written from positions of passionate involvement. In the first two, the writers deliberate the relevance of studying cultural traditions such as "Black" poetry or "Women's" poetry. Each of the next essays compares different poets whose work can be classified under a single, broadly-defined cultural tradition.

The essays are followed by "Assignment Poets" that continue to explore the relationship between the poet and his or her particular cultural legacy.

Shelly Smith
(photo by June Jordan)

Whitegirl Write Black Poem: On the Politics of Paleness   Shelly Smith

I enrolled in "Reading and Writing African American Poetry," one of the first pilot classes for Poetry for the People, on a whim, simply because I wanted to write poetry. At first I felt very uncomfortable because I am White, and much of me felt critical of my own presence in a space where African American students could and should freely explore their own cultural heritage. I worried that any attempt to write African American poetry on my part would be false and forced. Despite these reservations I kept going to the class because I was discovering poetry—the sound of it, the taste of it, the feel of it flowing out of my pen—and I didn't want to give it up.

Early in the semester I went to June's office to voice my concerns and to give her a chance to reject me from the class. I told her I feared mimicking a style of poetry which wasn't mine instead of writing from my heart. She looked at me over her glasses and said, "If I could learn to write poetry reading Shakespeare, you can learn to write poetry reading Paul Lawrence Dunbar." She told me to look everywhere, not just in the assigned reading material, for aspects of the African American experience that spoke to me personally and then to respond in my own way. Directing me to Susan Griffin's "I Like to Think of Harriet Tubman" as a good example of an African American poem written by a White woman, she said, "Ultimately you have to stop talking about it and worrying about it and start doing it."

So I read a lot and I listened a lot and I looked inside myself and discovered I had a lot to say. We had an assignment to write a poem in the style of or in response to one written by Ntozake Shange. I read Shange out loud for days, just letting her rhythms and tones sink in. Then I started to write, and the next thing I knew I had a Shange-style poem, full of love and natural imagery and sex and politics, which was nonetheless all my own. (Shelly Smith's "A Love Poem for George Bush" appears in Chapter 10.)

Shelly Smith *fantasizes about someday opening her mouth and having a brilliant bass line or a breathtaking flute solo emerge instead of words. Barring that, she hopes to learn to play the guitar sometime.*

Thoughts on Poetry and Women's Culture   Leslie Shown

My next door neighbor's name is Walter. He is eighty-six years old, and lost his
wife of more than sixty years on my thirtieth birthday last May, a day when
everyone who loves me and lives within driving distance fed me, sang to me,
imagined with me how rich the next thirty years will be, and held me in their
arms. Walt is only beginning to emerge from the dark place of grief, and
sometimes tells me that I saved his life by being kind to him and listening to
his stories.

A few weeks ago, Walt called to ask if I would stop by and in the evening I
walked next door for a visit. We sat in the two easy chairs in his living room,
and he showed me the beautiful eulogy that he had written for his wife's
funeral and a copy of his tax returns for the previous year. He pointed out an
itemized list of more than $30,000 in donations to organizations like Women
Against Rape, Mothers Against Drunk Driving, and Greenpeace, and he asked
me if I could see how hard he was trying to win my approval. I looked at him
with surprise, and reassured him that he already had my approval. He looked
relieved and said that he had thought I was angry, that he thought I had
become upset because I knew he was watching me. Thus I learned that Walt
can see into my kitchen and living room from the room in his basement he
calls his laboratory. He watches me cook; he watches me as I sit at my table
and read and write; he says he stays alive by watching someone who is so
vibrantly alive. But he felt it was wrong and so did I, and we made an
agreement that he would not watch me anymore.

I fell asleep that night trying to believe that it is perfectly understandable
for a lonely old man who recently lost his wife to stand in the dark of his
basement to watch a young woman cook and read. I fell asleep trying to
remember that we live in a culture where old people are severely isolated,
deprived of human contact and comfort, and that Walt was trying to stay alive
the only way he knew how. I fell asleep trying to trust that Walt would never
hurt me, that the wind rustling the bushes outside my bedroom window was
not in fact my neighbor, and that his invasion of my private life was in no way
sexual oppression. I fell asleep and I dreamed that I raped my friend Sylvia, a
lesbian who was molested as a child and has never had sex with a man.

I woke up more frightened from the dream of raping a woman than I
have ever been of a man in my waking life. I walked through the next half-
week in a daze, trying to understand what the dream meant, and what
violence I might be capable of. At last, I decided that this dream was not
about my potential for violence but my potential for denial. I realized that my
nightmare was was an unconscious response to how hard I wanted to

convince myself of the harmlessness of Walt's intentions and how hard I was struggling to forgive him for watching me. I so much wanted to love and accept my neighbor that in my dream I became him; I so much wanted to love my neighbor because I am so tired of being silently angry and afraid.

Perhaps the connection of this story to women's culture and poetry is not immediately apparent; but, for me, the connection is profound. Like so many girls, I was raised to be kind and empathetic, to give everyone the benefit of the doubt. I was taught that the best way to be a good sister/daughter/wife/mother/lover is to comply. I was taught that what might feel like sexual oppression was nothing more than a product of my oversensitivity and that rape was something that happened to bad girls. I was taught to love my neighbor—even if he is a man who watches me from his basement.

I believe that the craziness that comes with trying to believe these cultural messages about how women are and should be is a powerful part of what defines a women's culture. As I have begun to write poems, and to read the poetry of other women, I have found that the process of sharing the previously unarticulated anger, fear, and sometimes pleasure of women's reality validates an entirely new realm of my life experience. The process of telling the truth about my life has replaced the nightmare in which I am trying so hard to love my oppressor that I become him. The process of discovering an unedited version of myself through writing poetry, and reading the poetry of other women, is the most pleasurable form of survival I have known.

from *Innovation and Experience:*
Li-Young Lee's "The City in Which I Love You"
and Donna Masini's "That Kind of Danger" Alegria Barclay

Both Lee and Masini write extensively about their fathers. Lee's tie to his father is empathic in its probing pain and tenderness. His father embodies what Lee struggles to remember: his Chinese ancestry, his people's suffering, the history so many try to forget. And yet, in "This Hour and What is Dead" this father "mends ten holes in the knees of five pairs of boy's pants." Lee juxtaposes beautifully the immensity of his father's ancestry with the tenderness of his father's sewing.

Masini finds a reason for how she sees the world in the reality of the filthiness her father brings home. In "Hunger," her father of the dirt, the sweat of life offers an alternative to her mother's "teased hair and lipsticks,/ her shadows and powders and tears." Her mother tries to give her make-up and make-overs, dresses and dolls, but cannot keep the soot from seeping into her daughter. In "Who Giveth This Woman," Masini drinks the dirt so that she "can feel the greased heat, underground boiling / rumblings in the tunnels of me."

The use of imagery in these poets' works is impressive and so, so beautiful. Some phrases never leave your head, like "Night is a skin / tough and coarse, porous as citrus peel" in Masini's "Girl, Gingerpot, Tree." Their imagery haunts us. Lee's imagery carries his poetry along. In "The Cleaving," the power of repetition propels us from line to line, from stanza to stanza, such as "the noise the body makes / when the body meets / the soul over the soul's ocean and penumbra / is the old sound of up-and-down, in-and-out,/a lump of muscle chug-chugging blood/ into the ear; a lover's/ heart-shaped tongue," and on and on. The music sustaining the metaphor flows throughout the poem, linking each word, each thought to the next. The poet relies less on actual rhythm than on the extension of one image throughout the whole poem, like a continuous note. Masini is less continuous with her imagery. It comes in waves, in short dashes, in lists of things that move with the rhythm of the city. It is less metaphorical and in some ways more effective in its vivid directness. In "Giants in the Earth," she writes "steel pipes like metal pelvises scattered across pavement, / the banging of tools falling in a strange blue light." Like most of her visions, this image is not easily shaken from your mind.

Lee and Masini differ in their manner of truth-telling, yet both invoke personal experience to part from tradition. Their poetry speaks with a beauty bred of passion and persistence.

from *No Time for Rhetoric*   Ananda Esteva

The difference between poetry and rhetoric
is being
ready to kill
yourself
instead of your children
—Audre Lorde

What is this thing called rhetoric? My dictionary described it as "the art of
using words effectively (especially in essays)" and also as "containing elements
of artificial eloquence." I read Lorde's words as saying that poetry in its most
righteous form is not rhetoric. June Jordan has said time and again that
poetry is a means of telling the truth. I don't know of any truth falling under
the title of "artificial eloquence." Poetry, when used as a means of truth telling,
requires a more involved position. Truth-telling poems may pull back and
summarize. They may construct conclusions, but I suggest the truth-telling poet
writes with less distance and more involvement than the rhetorical poet.

Let me tell you, I nearly fell over when I reread that poem of Lorna Dee
Cervantes entitled, "Poem for the Young White Man Who Asked Me How I, an
Intelligent, Well-Read Person Could Believe in the War Between the Races." I
believe that poem cuts the edge of subversive. Yet, during the same period, a
Salvadoreña (also considered "Latina" in this country) named Martivón
Galindo wrote her poem, "Life Looks Different" about a similar issue. The voice
of a rich white male dictates the opening stanzas of both poems. While the
structures sit parallel, the languages stand worlds apart. Unfortunately, I can't
take the liberty to compare the intricacies of the poets' languages because the
Galindo poem has been translated into English. Despite the nuances veiled by
the translation, the level of involvement is clear. While both poets scorn the
social remoteness earned by the upper classes, Cervantes writes at a distance
(most likely) inaccessible to Galindo.

In "Poem for the Young White Man," Lorna Dee Cervantes unravels some of
the social effects of institutionalized racism in the U.S. First she utilizes the
voice of a liberal and racist white man. "In my land there are no distinctions,"
he says, and that is precisely the point that she contests. She then lists some
social problems: "everywhere the crosses are burning, / sharp-shooting goose-
steppers around every corner / there are snipers in the schools..." She
mentions these situations as though she were reading the headlines of a
newspaper. She has done better than the white man in this poem, at least she
can define some problems in the third person. Galindo never uses the third

person. She uses her own voice to describe and define her gripes: "I am not a clay doll from Llobasco / Don't watch me from a distance..." Surely there are not burning crosses everywhere nor sharpshooters around every corner, but Cervantes uses this as a device, as part of a vision. Galindo uses the specific and the personal instead of the theoretical. Galindo wrote her poem right before the El Salvadorean Revolution, during a time when economic stratification screamed, severe and obvious. Cervantes' final line, "but in this country / there is war," is already understood in Galindo's poem....

Tomo O'Brien, editor of
**Poetry for the People:
What Now?**
(photo by June Jordan)

Assignment Poems

The following poem was written in response to the assignment to write a "How Do I Love Thee" poem, using Elizabeth Barrett Browning, Queen Latifah, and Toni Braxton as models.

untitled   Samiya A. Bashir

How do I love you? Let me count the ways…
you ever stand on top of a cliff over the ocean
in a misty morning sunrise, or
        swim naked in a cool still lake on a hot afternoon in July, or
                fall asleep in the sunrise after making love all night long
no, no don't misunderstand
my love for you is more than all of these things
I love you like a bird flying north in the springtime
                instinctively
you encompass me like the earth its core and
        loving you is all I wanna do
I can't eat baby
        I can't sleep
                I lay in bed all day just to smell you on my sheets
I can't even watch cartoons on t.v.
        they've all got your face
How come the papers
        have no mention of my love for you
How come the news don't show your picture at least
                                                once an hour
Baby my love for you makes the
world turn on its axis
        makes the sun redhot
                the stars shine
                        the moon glow and
                                rabbits taste just like chicken
                                        cuz of you

If you asked me to I wouldn't climb the highest mountain
    I'd build it
I wouldn't sail the widest sea
    I'd drink it
        just to give you the beach to lie on
How do I love you?

Baby there ain't enough math in the world for me to
count the ways
    ain't enough music to sing 'em
        ain't enough colors to paint 'em
            ain't enough words to say 'em
                baby
even this poetry falls short of my love for you
which is taller than a redwood reaching up to the sky
    my love is delirious from lack of oxygen
it makes my blood so hot, I'm running a fever of 104
    n ain't no way Tylenol counted on this cuz
               there ain't no cure for my love
                  but you

ain't no safe haven where I can hide cuz
        it eats me up like greens n biscuits on Sunday afternoon
        from the inside
            but
        mmmmm you taste good
I can't count the ways I love you
but I'd try if you asked me I'd
    make up a new language to speak it in cuz
          this one don't work
How do I love you?
        too much to waste this time counting...
              let me show you.

This poem was inspired by Joy Harjo's "I Give You Back" (*She Had Some Horses*, 1983).

I Own You Now

maiana minahal

i own you now / my anger,
my once-blinding sickness,
my nightmare with no name.
you bind me no longer.
once i choked on hail marys,
told to vomit you out
into the bottle
i should cap and keep hidden
the wrong way to purge you.
instead / inside me still,
you grew / parasitic tumor,
eating up my insides.
then you tore through my flesh
and lashed me to a rack,
stretching me like a sheet
so tight and taut
that i almost know myself no longer,

almost becoming some self
that wants to smash the bottle
and with the shards
carve up someone's face / anyone's
even my face.
now,
when i want,
i will reach down,
pull you out
and smash your face against concrete,
and watch you,
you small / sniveling mass,
wither away in the sun.

This poem was inspired by Li-Young Lee's "This Room and Everything in
It" (*The City in Which I Love You*, 1990).

Pop   Albert Tong

i lie
in the breaking quiet
listening to my father as he wakes to
whispers of a worn flannel shirt and
the muted chime of a belt already on
dark brown corduroys
walking footsteps
out the kitchen door

this house this place
an ocean away from where he lay years ago
listening to his father wake
leaving what he knew
and arriving into what he did not
the master of his universe so
lost in another

and his hands
deep rough grooved
blackened oil and grease trapped in his nails
blisters scarred from solder
hands that are strong delicate skilled
hands that hold mine
protect mine keep mine
soft smooth ignorant

and so i lie
sheltered in a bed of his quiet watch
in a house that protects me from bitter evils
that i do not care
or want
or will ever see
in a place that mocks him, beats him, rapes him
away from his bed, his house, his place

After the class read E. Ethelbert Miller's "Separation Demands That All Things Be Reduced to Pieces" (*First Light New and Selected Poems*, 1994), June gave an assignment to write a poem portraying an act of physical violence. Jennifer Lim wrote the following poem in response to the brutal murder of Vincent Chin, a Chinese American kicked and bludgeoned to death with a baseball bat. Chin's killers were tried and released on probation, with a fine of $3780 each. Mistaking his victim as Japanese, one of the killers was overheard in court saying, "It's because of you motherfuckers I'm out of a job." He is the subject of the poem.

Ebens   Jennifer Lim

>   I take you out to the ball park
>   One swing. Knees meet pavement
>   Red rain sprinkles lightly on my cheek
>   Second swing. Neck snaps with a crack
>   Damn (thought I broke the bat)
>   Third swing. Head explodes into a double
>
>   Rolling on the ground
>   My smug smile brightens
>   The gloom of the day
>
>   "It could happen to anyone,"
>   Your words echo in my ear
>   This time I guess it's you

The question "Where Are We and Whose Country Is This Anyway?" elicited
the following poems.

Where Is My Country?   Xochiquetzal Candelaria

    my country dances through los angeles
    downtown
    smelling like mexico city
    cuz sidewalk sales spread aromas of
    tamales
    perfume
    new shoes

    a five year old girl wipes mango pulp
    on her sleeve
    to show her grandma una boca limpia
    while three boys push by
    tackling each other

    musica ranchera encircles everyone

    but for how long
    when city hall calls downtown
    dangerous and dirty
    cuz fruit doesn't come wrapped in plastic
    and not enough visa cards charge

    when spanish can't be spoken
    without a wet back
    cuz a gang of white boys might take
    the law into their own hands

    when a chicana knows
    her light skin saves her
    ass

i reply
this country dances
as long as people
in mexico, guatemala, el salvador, nicaragua
panama
down to the tip of argentina
keep discovering us
over and over again

this country dances
as long as i keep the beat
when a mother or a brother
needs to rest

Portrait of a Minority Masterpiece in the Making

Junichi P. Semitsu

On opening night
Our people-of-color productions will paint portraits
of manifest destineo-nazi genocide!
Settlers provide small-pox infested clothes while millions
decompose in reservation graves
Slave ship captains throw black bone scraps in the Atlantic abyss
Prejudiced farmowners kill pregnant Mexican mothers already ill
from pesticide countrysides
Dissatisfied workers bash Asian bodies with wooden bats
to combat unemployment
The unenjoyment under these stars and stripes writes this scary
yet revolutionary text of tyranny,
But hear ye: critics condemn us as un-American
And the show cannot go on.

Instead
We perform portraits of strong ethnic pride!
Get funkdafied to the fire of James Baldwin and the soul
of James Brown
Cheer striking women's slowdowns in New York Chinatown
Rejoice in the melody of Mayan prayer and the laws
from the Iroquois
Applaud the resistance of Cesar and the persistence
of trans-continental boys
Our voice reflects all the bright colors in the rainbow of America,
But let me tell ya: critics condemn these separatist sentiments
And we can't fill the first five rows.

So
We sketch portraits of pretty picture brides!
Natives practice backward religions with peyote spirits narcotic
Exotic mail-order women submit to sadistic demands of opium
orientals
Ethiopian Kunta Kentals fall prey to their jungle-like libido

131

As we see those savage Sambos and weak Korean Rambos
fight each other at last
with a supporting cast of uncivilized scalping Choctaws,
                sneaky spying Kamikazes,
                lazy Latino looters
The thick-accented cast tells jokes of Filipino hooters
big lips, cheese nips, and well-equipped black prickets
The audience (who can afford the $50 tickets) leaves feeling great
And critics salivate and proclaim this piece fresh
And we fill almost every seat on the floor.
Therefore
We scrap portraits of any third world strides!
In a slapstick salute to heathen heritage
Charlie Chan, Aunt Jemima, Juan Valdéz,
and the Redskins reunitin'
We hire Michael Crichton for the ethnic writin'
McDonalds Happy Meal(TM)-izes and capitalizes
with collectible fightin' action-figure winos

Cameron Mackintosh directs the all albino
cast starring action-figure winos
Ted Blackface Danson and the handsome Dukes of Hazzard hicks
    and Walt Disney picks
      up the rights to the theme park...

Then hark!
The Herald critics will declare this minstrel show a true
American art form
    and then finally we can perform
        then scream and shout:
"We sold every ticket! God damn it, we sold out!"

Part Two

TAKING POETRY BACK
TO THE PEOPLE

Albert Tong

Erskine Peters, Poetry for the People
guest lecturer, Professor of English,
Notre Dame University

The poets of Poetry for the
People, Spring 1995

Xochiquetzal Candelaria
and guest poet
Donna Masini

Debbie Miller

(all photos by June Jordan)

6

WORD OF MOUTH
Staging A Revolutionary Reading

Poetry Should Ride The Bus   Ruth Forman

> poetry should hopscotch in a polka dot dress
> wheel cartwheels
> n hold your hand
> when you walk past the yellow crackhouse
>
> poetry should wear bright red lipstick
> n practice kisses in the mirror
> for all the fine young men with fades
> shootin craps around the corner
>
> poetry should dress in fine plum linen suits
> n not be so educated that it don't stop in
> every now n then to sit on the porch
> and talk about the comins and goins of the world
>
> poetry should ride the bus
> in a fat woman's Safeway bag
> between the greens n chicken wings
> to be served with tuesday's dinner

poetry should drop by a sweet potato pie
ask about the grandchildren
n sit through a whole photo album
on an orange plastic covered lazyboy with no place to go

poetry should sing red revolution love songs
that massage your scalp
and bring hope to your blood
when you think you're too old to fight

yep
poetry should whisper electric blue magic
all the years of your life
never forgettin to look you in the soul
every once in a while
n smile

The poets of **Poetry for the People in a Time of War**.
(photo by Deirdre Visser)

GETTING OUR VOICES OUT THERE

Poetry read aloud to a room full of people gathered in expectancy and celebration becomes a growing thing. Poetry read aloud becomes an *event*: dynamic, fluid, changing from moment to moment, from poet to poet. Sitting through three hours of poetry, soaking in power-packed testimonies, poets and listeners together hum high energy. Smatterings of applause, hushes, bursts of laughter, call and response, and standing ovations bridge the silence of mutual fear or indifference. Each reaction from the audience feeds the poets and creates new poems that never appear on a printed page.

Candles and Poetry   Rubén Antonio Villalobos

Confessing your love to someone can be difficult. Doing it in front of three hundred people is downright mortifying. Last year, like a typical forgetful guy, I scheduled myself to work the nightshift on Valentine's Day. Although I remedied this February fourteenth faux pas by cooking a candlelight dinner, I was still in dangerous waters. Flowers would not work. This called for something special, and Cupid didn't seem to be helping.

Last semester's reading, Poetry for the People in a Season of Love, proved the perfect opportunity. Let me tell you, that night I felt like a poet. I came in true poet's garb: a dress jacket over a black turtleneck, jeans, argyles, and of course, Birkenstocks. Just as I finished my first poem, Cupid struck! Instead of reading the poem I had planned to read next, I read a poem that I wrote to my girlfriend (who had complained that I wrote about everything but her!). I looked straight at her, and introduced the poem by telling the audience that the next poem was for my girlfriend, but that they were free to listen. As I read the poem I thought, Oh my God! This is either going to be terribly corny or extremely romantic. It turned out to be both, and when I looked up from the poem, I noticed that mine were not the only wet eyes in the room. My girlfriend was extremely flattered, and all of her friends kidded (and congratulated) her for days to come. After that poem, my Valentine's Day blunder was forgotten!

The Personal as Universal

Jin Kyoung Jun

As I walk, nervous and unsure, towards the mike, I recall June's advice, "Just say it from your gut, be honest." My first few words stumble and spill from my lips as I stand before a faceless crowd. Thoughts run through my mind: What do they want? Why are they here? Most importantly, will they listen, will they hear me?

My poem begins in my mother tongue, Korean, "Aboji, you say to me miguk un cho ji an na." I express the dehumanizing cultural and linguistic rape I underwent in America and its educational institutions upon immigrating here. I challenge America's standards of race and ethnicity and deconstruct the myth of the "model minority." In my poem, I state how "if you're not white, you're not quite." At that, an African American male with dreds and a colorful hat cries, "Right on," as he rises from his chair and twirls his fist. Another voice shouts, "You tell it girl," and my voice and mind and heart gain momentum, strength, power... applause. I'm back on the ground again. The rush ends, or so I think....

The next day, three complete strangers approach me in response to my poem. An Asian American female student introduces herself, shakes my hand, looks into my eyes and says, "Thank you for your poem" in such a way it gives me chills. Walking on campus the same day, a Chicano student brushes past me, patting me on the shoulder saying, "That was a fucking awesome poem!" A White female student compliments, "You were great last night. My best friend is Korean American and your poem made me rethink the differences in our experiences."

A little dazed and awed I have a flashback, the image of June lifting her two thumbs at me with a smile, and I realize the rush continues, past me and through others.

(The poem Jin Kyoung Jun read that night appears in Chapter 10.)

PREPARING FOR THE BIG EVENTS

Our free student readings feature thirty to forty poets, many of whom are reading poetry for the first time in their lives. Always electric, these events are standing room only and draw from 100 to 300 people. Reading poetry to an audience for the first time can be quite scary. When the class first hears they are required to do a reading at the end of the semester, many students cringe or protest, or begin to plan the illness they will mysteriously come down with that day. So we practice. In our writing groups we give each other constructive criticism and discuss general presentation tips. Student teachers hold office hours to give individual poets one-on-one attention. Before class lecture, we hold a twenty-minute open mike so writers can present their poems in front of the entire collective. Finally, before each reading we hold a rehearsal where poets can test the microphone, time themselves, and become familiar with the room's acoustics.

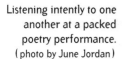

Listening intently to one another at a packed poetry performance. (photo by June Jordan)

On Performing Your Poetry for the First Time   Shelly Smith

The first time I ever read I felt like I was literally going to die when I walked on that stage. I even had trouble reading aloud to people in my class. An actress friend of mine did exercises with me to get me a little more comfortable reading. I practiced reading in whispers and shouting angrily and like I was about to cry, just to get comfortable with the range of possibilities. Then she told me to focus on what I was feeling when I wrote the poem and to read it that way. When I really brought myself back to the moment I wrote it, and read it with those feelings, I read it best. I recited it in the shower, as I was riding my bike, in empty classrooms. When the time came to read publicly, I was so familiar with the words that they carried me; in the midst of all that terror I felt a pleasure that my words sounded good and that I could trust them to carry me through this experience.

The following tips will aid the first-time reader: The number one rule for reading is *low and slow*. Keep these two words in your head as you walk up to that mike. Nervousness tends to make a person's voice about two octaves higher than normal and makes him/her read about twice as fast. Before the event, read your poem aloud to as many people as you can. This ups your confidence and helps you clear up awkward parts of your poem. Practice speaking loudly, from your diaphragm, so your voice projects to the back of the room. A good exercise for projection is to say vowel sounds (ah! ee! ay! oh! oo!) with force, like you're launching missiles out of your mouth. You can experiment with body language and intonation, too, but don't let it distract you from reading your poem clearly, slowly, and loudly enough for people to hear you. Expect to pause for audience response after certain especially fresh lines. Avoid beginning your reading with long introductions, apologies, or the deadly: "this poem is about...." Let your poem do the talking. Keep your energy level high (don't forget to breathe), and if you make a mistake, just keep going!

Settin' Up the Place

1. *A Room for the Reading*: To honor the poets and the audience, secure the most beautiful space possible. Book the room early and note any preexisting damage so you won't be billed for it. We usually decorate the room with flowers; one semester we borrowed a backdrop from the English department to spiff up the stage. We also reserve seats for the poets.

2. *Technical Details*: If lighting is available, ask the technician to place spotlights on readers and turn the house lights down; this makes the space warmer and more intimate. Also let the technician know if you have an intermission or an interpreter for the deaf. ASL interpreters require early notice and charge approximately $40 per hour. Remember that poets who use a wheelchair need stage access, and the room itself should be wheelchair accessible to the audience. We record all of our readings ourselves, but most campuses have an office of media services that can film the readings, usually for less than $20 per hour. When possible, we record sound directly from the main microphone. This makes a huge difference in sound quality, if done correctly. (One year, we did it wrong and ended up with a silent film, so you should probably conduct a test recording.) We then archive the tapes in our developing Poetry Center library. These tapes are used by individual poets who want to critique their presentation styles and in poetry workshops to get pumped for our next readings.

3. *Programs*: We design our own programs on a computer and then have them printed on resumé-grade paper. This costs approximately $15 for three hundred programs. The program cover lists "what," "where," and "when" information, while the inside presents our mission and lists the poets alphabetically. We save the back to acknowledge sponsors, campus big shots and guest poets. The printer needs a day to produce the programs. We get the folding done in fifteen minutes, so we put it off until the night before the reading. Getting the program ready well in advance doesn't work for us because of last-minute changes in the poet list or with the sponsors.

4. *Extra Touches*: A local flower store donates a few bouquets for the stage at almost every reading. As guests arrive, ushers seat them, starting near the front of the room. A student MC introduces the reading and acknowledges our sponsors. We prepare a list of the poets ahead of time, and each poet introduces "the next fantabulous poet." Finally, we have ice water and cups available for the poets.

Benefits

Recently we've begun to use our readings as benefits for other members of our local and global community. We set up tables outside the room where the reading takes place to sell Poetry for the People anthologies and posters. We also make a couple of hundred dollars passing the hat. At our reading *Poetry for the People In a Time of Genocide*, we raised donations for the International Rescue Committee and the Women's Coalition on Ethnic Cleansing, two organizations providing relief in war-torn Bosnia. Our reading *Poetry for the People In a Season of Love* benefited our poetry outreach program at Manzanita and Highland Elementary Schools in Oakland. If you're planning a benefit, get the word out! Businesses will donate goods and services if you explain the charity. Provide businesses with specific ways they can help, and remind them that their donations are tax deductible and that you will advertise their support on flyers and programs pertaining to the reading. Most institutions have regulations making it virtually impossible to hold a benefit unless it's planned way in advance, so start early.

Poetry in a Time of Genocide
A Benefit for the Victims of Ethnic Cleansing in former Yugoslavia

Yes, I want to help the survivors in
Bosnia-Herçegovina by contributing $ _____
☐ cash ☐ check (check one) to the Women's
Coalition Against Ethnic Cleansing and the
International Rescue Committee (Make checks
payable to Poetry for the People, memo: End
Genocide).

For a donation of $10.00 or more you receive a voucher for the
anthology: POETRY in a TIME of GENOCIDE
(See voucher for further instructions)

Name:_____

Phone:_____

# of anthologies:_____

Donations may be mailed by November 24, 1993 to:
Poetry for the People
c/o June Jordan
354 Dwinelle
Berkeley, CA 94720

A sample donation sheet from our **Poetry in a Time of Genocide** reading.

HOT SHOT POET READINGS

Poetry for the People also hosts free readings by America's leading poets. Drawing hundreds of people from the university and the outlying communities, these readings confirm the need to celebrate poetry as a communal, oral art form. We, the audience, collaborate with the poet in creating an event that benefits us all; we come away with expanded visions and new hopes. We hear our struggles articulated and respond vociferously. When Ntozake Shange read to a packed house of 750 a few years ago, she incorporated dance, theater, and her deep love of jazz into a performance (and it *was* a performance) that left the audience exhilarated. A year later, Joy Harjo stood in the same spot just a few days after the 500th anniversary of Columbus' arrival in North America and read of her experiences as a Native American woman in a society devoted to eliminating her people. Many came away with a deeper understanding of this holiday which our country had so glibly celebrated. These respected poets articulate our dreams and our rage and send us away with new visions of the poetic potential of our own lives.

Once you confirm a poet or guest lecturer, the behind-the-scenes work begins. Arranging airfare, hotel, car rental, parking, and honorarium requires a great deal of work. The following suggestions should make this process easier.

Hot Shot Poet Cornelius Eady after his magnificent reading. April 4, 1995. (photo by June Jordan)

Guest Presentation Checklist

1. Making Arrangements:
   a. Find out if your campus/institution has any set procedures in this area.
   b. Speak to the managers of local bookstores, as publishers sometimes pay expenses if a book sale is arranged in conjunction with the lecture. That way, you don't have to pay!
   c. Airlines and local hotels may donate their services if you send them a letter explaining your program. If the guest poet needs a rental car, she or he should rent the car and get reimbursed because rental agencies require specific insurance information from the driver.
   d. Offer whatever you can afford as an honorarium to the poet.
2. Before the Reading:
   a. Welcome the poet by meeting her or him at the airport. You can also arrange a reception or meal in her or his honor.
   b. Look over the poet's curriculum vitae (resumé) ahead of time so that you can introduce her or him properly.
   c. Before the poet reads, ask if she or he would prefer a podium with a microphone or a free standing mike.
   d. Have a pitcher of ice water and a glass nearby.
   e. Always get the guest poet's permission before videotaping her or him.
3. Afterwards: Send a thank you letter.

CHILLIN' AFTER (OR BEFORE) THE READINGS

Whether it's a Hot Shot Poet reading or a student reading, we hold a reception/feast/celebration with refreshments ranging from polenta to pizza to chocolate-covered strawberries to Samiya's Somali/tamale dish to salads o'plenty to falafel to enchiladas to bagels and more. We fill the room with drink, music, dancing, freestyle rapping, hugging, many compliments, and much release. We celebrate each other, then ask: "Can we do it again tomorrow?"

Reception Timeline and Checklist

Six Weeks Before Reception:
Reserve reception room and plan reception expenses into your budget. Estimate the number of people you want to feed. We usually invite the poets and their guests, campus big shots, and people from businesses that have donated food or supplies for the reception. If volunteers (poets not reading that night) bring their favorite dishes, the variety and quality of food that shows up rivals any donations we could get from *anywhere*. (Those poets who aren't reading that night cook, and those who are reading concentrate on being nervous.) If, however, your group is not providing the food itself, decide what food and items need to be donated or purchased. Most businesses will only donate a small amount, so send solicitation letters to more donors than you need. In the letter, explain the event and say that you will advertise the business in the program. If possible, all letters should be on official organization letterhead.

Four Weeks Before Reception:
Follow up letters with a personal phone call to donors. Have a list of goods and services desired. If businesses agree to contribute, send a thank-you letter to confirm the worth of the donation for their records. Honor them with an invitation to the event.

One Week Before Reception:
Circulate a sign-up sheet a week before the reading, encouraging people to bring culturally diverse and yummy foods. Call donors with last-minute reminders, and pick up non-perishable goods. Buy any necessary supplies that you can't get for free.

Day of the Reception:
Pick up all remaining donations. Remember the easily forgettable: trash bags, napkins, bottle openers, and so on. Set up tables with table cloths and candles, prepare food (cut bread, put food on serving platter, start coffee and tea, etc.), arrange food and flowers, get ice. Above all, don't forget the music!

After the Reception:
Keep playing the music as you clean up. Split up the leftover food or give it to the homeless. Arrange for people to pick up their plates after the reading. Vacuum the floors and clean the kitchen. Everyone should help clean, but people tend to flake out, so plan a clean-up committee ahead of time.

June. Lauren. and Amigo chillin' after (or before) the readings. (photo by Ariel Muller)

Into Open Arms and Handshakes   Shelly Teves

I brought store-bought cookies, the chewy, nonfat, nondairy, nondescript kind.
Made with organic grains and sweetened with fruit juice, they taste the same
regardless of the proclaimed flavor printed on the package. I purchased four
boxes of these cookies for the postreading reception. I brought them into the
student lounge, deposited them on a table, and wandered off in a rapidly
accelerating adrenaline rush that insisted on an absolute and complete
dilation of everything to accommodate its surge. Blood vessels, windpipes,
eyelids, pupils, and pores, throbbed open as I headed down the hallway,
reminding myself to breathe deeply.

Inside the Maude Fife room, I examined the program and saw my name
listed with thirty-six others under the heading "Poets." Everyone on that list
had access to one of June's two college classes: "The Art of Teaching and
Writing Poetry" or "Coming into the World Female." Clearly the privilege of
that access alone limited our diversity. Nonetheless, the poems took us to
places like Taiwan in 1944, where we followed a poet's grandmother,
"daughter strapped to back / two in hand" as she "dodges bombs—made in
u.s.a." (Jane Chen, "Ah-ma Ti"). We visited White middle-class statusville
where "cereals always stay afloat / space shuttles don't drop / hubba bubba
b-b-bubbles don't stick / when they pop" (Sean Lewis, "Abusive
Relationships"). We even surveyed "the lesbianscape / where loaded lockets
and leftovers / get lobbed at lords and ladies in the lobby" (cha, "lex,
love/lust of my life").

Each poet who stepped to the podium lifted the lid of a carefully crafted
container that made my world bigger by opening my mind—the sweetest of
sensations. As one of many listeners, I gave every ounce of my attentive energy.
In return, I received a hundred percent and more, especially from the poets
writing of their mixed heritage. These poets unpacked and held up my own
nagging questions and contradictions about where I belong. They provoked
me to begin a much-needed soul and ancestor search.

As a poet reciting for the first time, all that attentive energy both aided and
intimidated me. I did not think of myself as a poet. I had almost zero
experience performing in public; I had never even spoken into a microphone
before. By the time my turn came, my head was buzzing with the words I
heard. Words that stripped me down naked and rubbed my skin raw. So
when I got to the podium and looked at the two hundred plus pairs of eyes
focused on my face, I lost myself, letting words pour out of my mouth. I then
returned to my seat, completely aware that I had experienced a
transformation, yet unaware of how well my performance had gone.

When the reading ended I felt dazed. The degree to which I had feared performing my poems was matched by the degree to which reciting them made me high. So I stumbled, startled, out of the Maude Fife room and into open arms, handshakes, and introductions. In no time at all I found myself quite at home in my poetry-induced stupor. Soon everyone was intoxicated with poetry, fine food, and/or beer. The student lounge swung that night like it never had before. The people lingered so long after closing that they had to be escorted out by campus police, leaving hours of work for the clean-up committee. As a result, June instituted a new postreading reception policy: "no alcohol, no candles, no sleeping bags."

Likewise, I instituted my own personal postreading reception policy: no more store-bought cookies. For the reception for the next Poetry for the People reading, I found myself up to my elbows preparing a veganized (Westernized) version of pancit, a Filipino dish my dad makes. I cut out the chicken and shrimp, replacing them with seitan. I used organic veggies, rice noodles, soy sauce, and a little bit of oil. My dish spoke loudly of my life's mixed experiences, and the people munched down every last morsel.

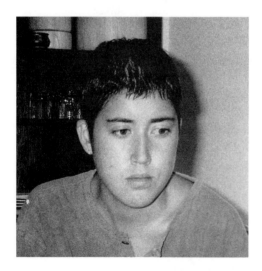

Shelly Teves
(photo by June Jordan)

7

PUBLICITY AND THE MEDIA
"Let Them Drink Nectar"

A reading packed with people hums honey down deep in bellies, buzzing boisterous in abdominal ears. We try to fill house and hive by working from the start of the semester, making flyers, contacting newspapers, radio and television stations, spreading the words like pollen.

Primarily, we buzz by word of mouth. Every poet in the collective takes responsibility for telling everyone he or she knows about the readings and bringing at least ten people. For the rest of the publicity work, we divide responsibilities between two different committees: on-campus media and off-campus media. Both groups choose one or two contact poets. These contact poets mark tasks on a calendar, keeping track of who takes on specific responsibilities and sometimes asking others in their committee to take on unclaimed jobs. The various jobs include creating and posting flyers and banners, tabling, making announcements in classrooms and departmental calendars, and sending out computer announcements, press releases, and invitations.

GETTING THE WORD OUT

Flyers

Flyers must be ready to go three weeks before the reading so we can mail them out as invitations. Our on-campus media committee asks the class to submit artwork for the flyer design. We try to make the flyer exciting, but simple enough to attract a wide audience. In previous semesters, we made all kinds of mistakes on the flyer—from mispelling one sponsor's name to leaving out the location of the reading. Just last semester, we made a flyer announcing: "Two Revolutionary Student Readings." Some people who saw this flyer thought that only two students were reading. To help avoid future mistakes on the flyer, we created the following checklist:

Flyer checklist
1. Remember to include the following information:
   a) Who, what, where, when
   b) Wheelchair Accessible
   c) Sign Interpreter and Childcare Available Upon Request (supply an office phone number)
   d) Bring Friends and Relations
   e) Printed on Recycled Paper/Please Recycle
   f) Faculty, "PLEASE ANNOUNCE"
   g) List of all sponsors
   h) Open to the Community
2. Submit the flyer for group review:
   a) Make sure the flyer represents everyone
   b) Make sure the flyer doesn't misrepresent anyone or the group as a whole
   c) Double-check the accuracy of information
3. Don't use one flyer for more than one date; people only pay attention to the first date.
4. Give the printers enough time to do their job. Ask for deadlines.

We use approximately 1,500–2,000 regular-sized flyers per reading of forty poets in a space that seats three hundred. We also use about 1,200 quarter-page flyers printed on colored paper for handouts.

Next, we use every means possible to get the flyer printed inexpensively on recycled paper. Here are some ideas:

1. Poetry for the People uses a massive amount of paper for letters, memos, notes, and revising poems. Try to save all paper that still has one blank side and recycle it by printing your flyers on this "reused" paper.
2. Take recycled paper to friendly campus departments and beg. Small departments such as Women's Studies, Native American Studies and African American Studies often support us by photocopying flyers for free.
3. Seek paper and copying contributions from local copy stores.
4. Purchase recycled paper. Take it to the printer. Photocopy it yourselves.

Meeting the flyer checklist...almost!

WHOSE COUNTRY IS THIS, ANYWAY?

Come hear
June Jordan's Poetry for the People

Student Poets

answer back
with poetry

1st night
Wed. April 19 @ 7:30 pm
in Maude Fife Room,
315 Wheeler Hall

FREE & open to the public
Reception immediately after reading

Wheelchair accessible
Sign language interpreter & childcare
available upon request (642-2743)

2nd night Fri. April 21
Same time & place

Once we have the flyers, the on-campus media committee asks each poet to distribute them to all students and faculty on campus, in four waves:

1. Mid-week of the week before the reading.
2. End of the week before the reading.
3. Beginning of the week of the reading.
4. Day of the reading.

Each poet takes at least fifteen flyers, covering the most fruitful locations on campus: mailboxes of faculty and graduate student instructors in friendly departments; any and all posting places on campus (announcement boards, bulletin boards outside classrooms, departments and faculty offices); community bulletin boards in bookstores, record stores, grocery stores, cafés, and community centers; telephone poles and garbage cans along the street. We also carry quarter- and half-size flyers which we hand out to people, encouraging them to BRING FRIENDS AND RELATIONS! (the word of mouth mantra).

While every poet in the collective helps out with the distribution of flyers, the members of the two publicity committees make an extra effort to cover the Bay Area with announcements. The on-campus media committee focuses its energy on reaching the campus community of students and faculty. In addition to posting, we pass out the smaller flyers at on-campus events (i.e. guest poet readings, dance performances, political rallies). This committee also spreads the word on Sproul Plaza (a people-magnet spot), handing out flyers during "high-traffic hours" two days before the reading. Meanwhile, the off-campus media committee uses our media resources (listed later in the chapter) as a tool for discovering events where we can spread the word. For example, we attended the dedication of the Audre Lorde Room, at the Women's Building in San Francisco, where we handed out five hundred small flyers.

Banners

The on-campus media committee makes banners on long, wide sheets of
paper (3' x 7') announcing the readings. We take advantage of both the
popular meeting spots and those places with a high student traffic flow by
hanging the banners there (i.e. Dwinelle Plaza and Wheeler Plaza). Two days
prior to the reading, we display two smaller banners on the announcement
boards on upper Sproul Plaza.

Classroom Announcements

Each poet takes responsibility for announcing the readings in his or her
classes. Then the on-campus media committee makes a list of the potentially
interested classes in which we may not be represented. The poets from this
committee wait for the professors outside of their classrooms before each
class begins. They ask professors if we can visit their classes to announce the
reading and hand out small flyers. The off-campus media committee
generally helps out with this task, too.

Departmental Calendars

The on-campus media committee also contacts friendly departments one
month prior to the event and asks them to include our event in their
newsletters or calendars. To ensure clear communication between department
staff and poets, we leave them a contact name.

Tabling

People from all parts of campus congregate on Sproul Plaza during lunch
hours. Like other campus organizations, we set up a table on the plaza and
hang posters advertising the readings with all relevant information. We keep
flyers of every size on the table, though people seem to like the quarter size
best. Along with items available on a donation basis (i.e. Poetry for the People
posters), we sell all of the Poetry for the People student anthologies from
past semesters: *Power of the Word*, *What Now?*, *Poetry in a Time of War*,
Poetry in a Time of Genocide, and *Poetry in a Season of Love*.

Computer Announcements

In the future, we want to use e-mail, computer bulletin boards, and other computer technology to publicize our readings. The off-campus media committee plans to send e-mail announcements and to ask the campus computer centers to place announcements on Campus News. We also want to check organizations with list services, like Berkeley News, Multicultural Bisexual Lesbian and Gay Alliance, and the Townsend Center for the Humanities.

Mailing Out Invitations

Three weeks before the reading, the off-campus media committee sends out invitations to all of our guest speakers, campus administrators, and sponsors.

Press Releases

The off-campus media committee timetable needs to focus on press releases. Magazines and journals like *Poetry Flash* have an especially long lead time. So, three or four months before the reading, one of the poets on the committee gets in touch with all of the media resources to verify deadlines. Once we know these deadlines we contact newspapers, poetry magazines, radio and television stations on departmental or organizational letterhead. We follow up on each of these contacts with phone calls to make sure our announcement does not get lost in the paper shuffle.

We write three types of press releases:

1. *News Desks*. Newspapers require a release two weeks before the reading in order to list information in their calendars. They need another, one week before the event. They also require a phone call the week of the reading.
2. *Public Service Announcements (PSAs)*. We call each radio and television station for the following information:
   a. Deadline for making announcements (usually seven weeks before the reading)
   b. Criteria for a PSA
   c. Length of spot
   d. Mailing address or fax number, including name of a contact person
   e. Information about community calendars

Also, we call local cable stations. Often they provide PSA or Community Calendar sections free of charge.

3. *News Editors*. We contact the news editors of newspapers and radio
stations that cover feature, local news, and entertainment. We do this as
soon as possible since they might want to run a story or cover the actual
reading. We inquire about Public Access Time to find out if we can
broadcast readings. Each year, KPFA and KQED, our favorite stations,
try to work us into their broadcasting schedule. They often let us read on
the air before the reading.

To give you a more concrete idea of what all this entails, here's a sample list
of specific organizations we contact in the San Francisco Bay Area.

Newspapers:	Main #	Fax #	Attention:
Oakland Tribune	510-208-6300	510-208-6477	Lola Smallwood
S.F. Bay Times	415-626-8121	415-626-0629	Maxine Morris
S.F. Chronicle	415-777-1111	415-512-8196	Melanie Ramsey
S.F. Examiner	415-777-7850	415-777-2525	The City Desk
S.F. Weekly	415-541-0700	415-777-1839	Editorial Desk
Berkeley Voice	510-644-8208	510-644-1735	Calendar Editor
Mercury News	510-839-5321	510-790-7332	Calendar Editor
Montclarion	510-339-4060	510-339-4066	Scott
Parents Press	510-524-1602	510-524-0912	Lois Silvers
East Bay Express	510-540-7400	510-540-7700	Vicki Cameron
S.F. Bay Guardian	415-255-3100	415-255-8955	Henry Kumagai
Poetry Flash	510-525-5476	510-540-1057	Joyce Jenkins
The Berkeleyan	510-642-3734		Lyn Hunter

Radio:	Main #	Fax #	Attention:
KABL	510-893-9600	510-392-3299	Rudy Bessera
KALX	510-642-1111		Carol Harris
KFOG	415-543-1045	415-995-6867	Peter Finch
KFRC	415-951-2326	415-951-2326	PSAs
KGO	510-808-0810		PSAs
KJAZ	510-769-4800	510-769-4849	Connie Booth
KKIQ	510-455-4500	510-416-1211	Shawn DeAngelo
KNBR	415-995-6800	415-896-0965	Gimmy Parkli
KPFA	510-848-6767	510-848-3812	PSAs
KQED	415-553-2129	415-553-2241	Denise Julia

Television:	Main #	Fax #	Attention:
KFTL	510-632-5385	510-632-8943	Tina Montez
KPIX	415-765-8883	415-765-8994	Lena Sullivan
KPST	415-697-6682	415-697-1268	Jenny Chen
KQED	415-864-2000	415-553-2241	Denise Julia
KRON	415-441-4444	415-561-8066	PSAs
KTVU	510-874-0180		Community Affairs
KOFY	415-821-2020		Public Affairs
ABC	415-954-7926	415-954-7633	Community Affairs

UNIVERSITY OF CALIFORNIA, BERKELEY

BERKELEY · DAVIS · IRVINE · LOS ANGELES · RIVERSIDE · SAN DIEGO · SAN FRANCISCO   SANTA BARBARA · SANTA CRUZ

AFRICAN AMERICAN STUDIES
3335 DWINELLE HALL # 2572
BERKELEY, CALIFORNIA 94720-2572
TEL: (510) 642-7084
FAX: (510) 642-0318

To: KPFA
Fax: 848-3812

***

PRESS RELEASE: Please include the following event in your
community calendar, arts calendar, and/or other relevant locations.

***

June Jordan's "Poetry for the People" will be holding two
student-readings on the UC Berkeley campus. Poetry for the People,
the creation of poet and political activist June Jordan, holds annual
student readings that are among the most popular in the Bay Area,
regularly drawing Standing Room Only crowds. This year's readings
will be held on Tuesday and Thursday, April 18th and 20th, in 145
Dwinelle Hall on the UC Berkeley campus. The events are absolutely
free and open to the public, and everyone is welcome. Free Child
Care and ASL interpretation available upon request.
        Contact Poetry for the People at (510) 642-2743 or the African
American Studies Department at (510) 642-7084 for more
information.

Sample Public Service
Announcement

8

REACHING INWARD AND OUTWARD THROUGH POETRY

> Who really matter are these young people: these new lives: original, furious, gentle, broken, lyrical, strong, and summoning.
>
> —June Jordan, *The Voice of the Children*

Poetry for the People is spreading. Practically from its inception, members of the class have performed at local community centers, set up their own workshops, and just generally talked it up—on the bus, at the market, in bed. Recently, we organized two successful outreach programs—one at local elementary and high schools, and another at Glide Memorial Church in San Francisco. Although the focus of this chapter is on elementary and high school outreach, we also highlight other types of outreach we have done either on our own or as a group.

WRITING POETRY WITH CHILDREN

In January of 1994, we initiated a program to reach out to local elementary schools. We learned that every detail about visiting schools can be an emotional and political hot spot for a group trying to reach a consensus. Poetry contest or poetry reading? Assemblies or classrooms? One school or seven? Ultimately, we took the advice of Renata, who had tutored in the Oakland schools, and decided to hold poetry writing workshops in two schools. We looked for schools that especially needed volunteers. When student teacher poet Paul recommended Highland Elementary, Pam called Principal Riley, who found three classrooms for us to visit. Pam rallied the outreach group, which evolved weekly as people got sick, had midterms, fell in love, and left town. "Outreachers" include student teacher poets, first-time and long-time poets, never-taught-poetry-before-in-my-life poets, and Lisa, who just showed up at the door.

We started out working with second through sixth graders at Highland Elementary School and, later, Manzanita Elementary School in Oakland. Although we had a stack of children's poetry books, we didn't really know what to expect—from the kids, from ourselves, from the poetry. In all, we did workshops in six separate classrooms, visiting each once a week over a six week period. Always, the children's excitement, their voices, inspired us.

Pamela Wilson,
a Women's Studies
major, brought passion
and spirit to her
teaching of poetry in
Oakland schools.
(photo by June Jordan)

Why Do Outreach?

People live a poem every minute they spend in the world. Reaction, memory, and dream: these are the springs of poetry. And a four-year-old flows among them as fully as any adult.

—June Jordan

Gary Chandler

I do outreach for a lot of little reasons, a motley of experiences and dreams and influences. The children, of course, give me the most obvious reason to return week after week. One second grade class gives us "hugs"—more accurately, full-fledged frenzies—after every workshop. Walking through the schools, young poets hold our hands, demand piggyback rides, carry our supplies, give us presents—everything children do to make someone older feel pretty good.

The pleasure I receive from teaching sharply contrasts with the sadness and anger I feel toward the conditions in the schools we visit: no playgrounds, no music or art programs, over thirty students per class and entire schools and neighborhoods shouting out for the support and respect they deserve, but rarely receive. It's hard to ignore such need.

Stephanie Rose

Young poets speak out against the drugs, guns, and abuse that define their world. Like all of us, they need an outlet for their fears. They have the words, but are scared to express them. Poetry heals: it exposes the lies and fights back in nonviolent ways. It gives these kids the freedom to move beyond routine "assignments" and write for themselves. They write with a purity and potency I strive for in my own work. Poetry has shown these kids a safe place to discover their choices and proclaim them out loud.

Stephanie Rose *is a Women's Studies major, a transfer student, and a VW owner.*

Pamela Wilson

The hardest thing about talking to kids is that you can't fake it.

Preparation

We try to tailor our workshops to the cultural reality of each class. At Highland Elementary School in Oakland, most of the students are African American. There's also a mix of Chicana/o, Latina/o, White, Cambodian, and others. Manzanita has similar ethnicities, though Mien and Hmong students form the predominant ethnic groups. Students in our workshops speak Mien, Hmong, Laotian, Spanish, Cambodian, English, and other languages. Finding culturally diverse children's poetry in English is tough. We have some fabulous books of African American children's poetry, but finding Latina/o and Asian and Asian American poetry has been more difficult (see Chapter 4 for a bibliography). Cutting cultural corners can be pretty embarrassing. At Manzanita, we asked some of the kids to write poetry in Mien. Imagine how stupid we felt when a chorus of kids (and their teacher) pointed out that Mien isn't a written language!

We pore over books of children's poetry, watch the news, and talk to friends and teachers in search of writing workshop ideas. Occasionally we even think up new exercises right in the classroom. Each week, someone picks up anything related to the upcoming poetry exercise, from raspberries to rap. Someone else types and copies the class's poems from the week before. Then we hop in Steph's VW and hit the road. Although we'd like to, we don't always plan everything we will say, practice every poem that we read, rehearse every exercise we use. At heart, our visits to the schools are spontaneous: we write, we argue, we teach, we panic, we laugh, we get lucky, we flake out, we make it just in time, we completely forget, we work, we work, we work, and we love it.

Listen Up! Children's Poems and How They Came to Be

On our first day, six of us went to Highland Elementary School in Oakland, all a bit nervous, none knowing exactly what was about to happen. From that first "Well, here we go!" outside the door of Ms. Armstrong's Second grade classroom, we've learned some lessons on how (and how *not*) to get a bunch of kids excited about writing poetry.

We try to have at least three Poetry for the People teacher-poets in each classroom. If you have more than six student-teachers, you might try splitting up and visiting different classes. An hour and a half is definitely too long for a workshop with elementary school kids, half an hour is too short. Most schools have classes which last between forty-five minutes and an hour, which works fine for poetry workshops. It's a good idea to talk with the teacher about the best time to come in—crowd control becomes dangerous as soon as a wayward poetry workshop wanders into the time scheduled for Computer Center, or worse yet, Recess! We visit each classroom once a week, always at the same time. After a couple weeks, the children start to remember, and look forward to, the arrival of the "Poetry People."

We try to do two poetry "exercises" at each of our workshops. We take about ten to fifteen minutes to say hello, calm everyone down, and introduce the first exercise, usually by reading our own poetry or poems by published writers. The next fifteen minutes are for the children to write, followed by a ten to fifteen minute reading, in which they hop up and present what they wrote to the entire group. If we have time, we explain the next exercise, let the children write for fifteen minutes, and finish off the workshop with another reading. This structure varies depending on the class, the exercises, and sometimes even the weather.

Here are some of our more successful ideas for writing exercises, followed by a sampling of the children's poetry, all written in class in fifteen minutes or less.

"*Today they vote in South Africa*": We used this assignment on the first day of free elections in South Africa. We asked the students to think of something they have always wanted, but have known will be very hard to get, just as Black South Africans must have felt about voting. An exercise like this can open the writer's eyes to the possibilities for poetic subject matter and also help her identify a clear purpose for writing the poem (see Chapter 2, Guideline #3, for more on the importance of a clear purpose.)

"*The Color of My Skin*": In this exercise, we asked everyone to describe the color of their skin. Their tactile responses broke through stereotypical (non)descriptions of skin color. This exercise helps the poets to start making metaphorical leaps and to become more comfortable grounding their poetry in resonant details (see Chapter 2, Guideline #7c).

"*Music/Picture/Food Poems*": Live music, actual art, and fun food can inspire bright, detailed poems. One week, the class grooved with a 1920s Chicago Blues record Pam brought in. The next, we peered into a Georgia O'Keefe painting and a poster titled *Avenida de Cesar Chavez*, both donated by a local art store. Another week, we stopped by the farmer's market to pick up fleshy, colorful fruits and veggies: eggplant, strawberry, pineapple, watermelon, asparagus, gooseberry. Anything bright and bold that a writer can see, hear, taste, smell, or touch inspires poetry. Close examination of the shapes and colors of a painting or the texture of a piece of fruit encourages the use of "specific, resonant, and representative details" (see guideline #7c). As new poets describe "objects" in concrete, tangible ways, they begin to create metaphors and similes that describe (seemingly) less tangible ideas, like injustice, love, compassion, rage.

Poems from Manzanita and Highland Elementary Schools
Oakland, California, Spring 1994

Stinky Feet

me frens tink mi feet ar
stinki but i know me feet
take me ani wer in the world

Benjamin León
6th Grade, Ms. Scott
Manzanita Elementary

Graffitti don't have to match

but looking at it express
feelings:
colors splash everywhere.
Like a giant rainbow,
mixing itself up.
It whorls and swirls
everywhere in a blender.
Why does it have to be painted over?

Julia/Honey Saeturn
6th Grade, Ms. Scott
Manzanita Elementary

Today they are voting for me

in South Africa.
I will lock up Ms. Williams
until she gives me straight Es.
And I will deck Bill Clinton in the mouth.
And paint the White House black.
And take all the guns
and recycle the guns and get my money!

Justin Watson
4th Grade, Ms. Williams
Highland Elementary

My sunset skin is

like sands on beaches,
glow of lights
at nights,
half burn cupcakes,
peanut butter sandwiches,
my sunset skin reminds me of my birthplace
where I grew up
until I move.

Nai Yuan Saetern
6th Grade, Ms. Scott
Manzanita Elementary

The color of a wooden

ruler, that leads you
through the way.
  Maybe the ears of a
  teddy bear that listens
  to every secret of the
  world.
  The box that holds
  adventure,
of dark blonde curls bouncing in a ribbon the color of questions and
answers.

Julia/Honey Saeturn
6th Grade, Ms. Scott
Manzanita Elementary

bark of tree, tan, hard, rough, strong

peach, plumb, ripe, tastey, sweet
beach sands, wooden wall, small, sandy
ginger, hairy, watery, sticky, juicy

Meychiem Saechao
6th Grade, Ms. Scott
Manzanita Elementary

Rainbow Color

The colors spreading all over
the places makes me think about
how a daisy would looked if
every petals would have a different color.

Colors will splash all over
you if you get closer to them.

Standing there looking at these colors
makes me want to touch it.

Looking at the colors close up makes
me want to blurt out my feelings.

Meuy Saepharn
6th Grade, Ms. Scott
Manzanita Elementary

Lonely Nights

Lonely nights
and days
with no brothers
or sisters
to play.
Anxious
eyes
looking
at
me.
Lying on her mother's legs.
Dark days and nights.
with no one
except her dear old mother.

Nai Yuan Saetern
6th Grade, Ms. Scott
Manzanita Elementary

We ask the poets to read their poems aloud after every exercise. We never bear down on anyone who doesn't want to present his or her poem, and we make sure to clap and congratulate each poet who does. We lead discussions of children's poems and ask them to call out the words that sing to them. Once they know people want to hear what they have to say, there's no stopping them. Self-confidence becomes contagious.

Teacher feedback helps us figure out the mistakes we've made and the successes we can build on. Ms. Scott asked to hear more of our poetry, and we've noticed students feel more comfortable sharing their work if we share ours. It also helps us remember a basic principle of Poetry for the People: as we teach, we learn.

A Note on Privacy

Every poet who writes from the heart sometimes writes poems she or he may not feel like sharing with peers. Before beginning an exercise, we announce that anyone who writes something private can put an "X" on her or his paper. That poem will only be read by us. However, this can get out of hand. Many new poets write excellent poems but feel shy about sharing them, even when their poems aren't particularly intimate. We try to discourage using the privacy mark unless "you've really written something very secret."

As the children learn to trust us, some choose to share their secrets. They express grief, or anger, or tell stories that aren't safe to share in their everyday lives. One third grade girl whispered to a member of our group that her brother wouldn't stop kissing her. Other boys and girls have alluded to physical or sexual abuse in their poetry. Subsequently, we contacted the local child protection agencies for literature to prepare ourselves to identify and respond to signs of abuse. We know that we are not experts. We use our judgment and rely on the advice of people more experienced. It is our responsibility to report suspected child abuse to the student's teacher.

Fireman Wishes

Gary Chandler

Kids will wager "a million bucks" on who can stay underwater longer or run faster or whatever, but when some kid bets "a dollar"—one from his pocket— it's serious business. Many kids write about wonderfully impossible things, like "McDonalds in my backyard." But Gary Frazier (from Highland) wrote "Today they vote in South Africa./And someday I can be a fireman." Like the kid who bets a dollar, Gary is serious about this wish.

Thursdays

Gary Chandler with students
from Manzanita Elementary School

Blackberries bleed red
on fingers
popped into open mouths
Men play dice
while young poets
splash cupcake colors
in the setting sun

Black South African voters
promise
fireman wishes will come true.

Will sisters of peacock brothers
remember
Poetry People/tigers who can sing the Blues?

COMMUNITY WORKSHOPS, PERFORMANCES, AND OTHER TYPES OF OUTREACH

> From its roots, Poetry for the People can't help but to reach out, and it has, and it does, and it is, *right now*. As you read this book, you become a firsthand witness to the possibilities of outreach.
>
> —Shelly Smith

Outreach can mean anything from reading your poetry once a week to your elderly next-door neighbor, to forming a group of three people to read and discuss each other's work. You can assemble a performance ensemble or start a new program in the school where you teach. No kind or amount of outreach is insignificant. Every new connection strengthens a tradition of creating beauty from your own life and sharing it, and weakens the common perception of poetry as elitist or irrelevant. To that end, several poets have undertaken projects designed to perpetuate poetry.

Getting ready to ride to Glide on the first night, February 23, 1995.
(photo by June Jordan)

Glide Church Poets

In the spring of 1995, Poetry for the People organized its first non-academic community outreach project in a collaboration with Glide Memorial Church, in the Tenderloin neighborhood of San Francisco. Glide provided the aspiring poets a place to meet, dinner, and administrative support, and Poetry for the People provided the teachers and a curriculum. For six weeks, Student Teacher Poets gave the Glide poets practical advice to aid them in telling some very important and powerful stories of addiction, abuse, disappointment, courage and survival. At the end of the program we staged a joint student-teacher reading at Glide, attended by over a hundred people. Poetry for the People looks forward to writing with the Glide poets for the next few years.

Glide Memorial Church
poet Victoria Stith
(photo by June Jordan)

Getting So Much Back   Alegria Barclay

I walked into Glide knowing nothing of what it was about. It turned out to be one of the most wonderful places I had ever encountered. There were people from all walks of life: teachers, singers, gays, lesbians, recovering drug addicts. In my group I had a twelve-year-old girl and a seventy-year-old woman. The diversity was amazing! More so because these people came with a genuine desire to learn; they were eager to write. There were no units, grades, G.P.A.'s to worry about, just the thirst, the need to open up and express themselves. It was beautiful. I found myself wanting to come back on Sundays and see what else Glide had to offer. I felt almost selfish, wanting to give more and more to these gorgeous people, because I was getting *so* much back.

The distinguished poet
Janice Mirikitani,
President of Glide
Memorial Church in
San Francisco, and
coordinator of Poetry
for the People at
Glide Church.
(photo by June Jordan)

The Anasi Writer's Workshop

The Anasi Writer's Workshop in Los Angeles, coordinated by former Poetry for the People student Michael Datcher and attended by former students Ruth Forman and Jamal Holmes, provides a gathering space for the Black writing community. Members present new writing, talk about issues (political or personal) and have contact with the more established writers within the Black community. In their mission statement, they explain: "The Anasi Writer's Workshop provides a venue for Black youths to constructively express the frustrations of living a young Black life in Los Angeles, while learning about art and culture from more mature people in the community. This African tradition of passing down knowledge is the foundation on which the workshop is built. The workshop also tries hard to create dialogue between disparate groups within the Black community, especially in relation to class, gender, and sexual preference."

The workshop is divided into three primary components: Traditional, Featured, and Open. During the hour-long Traditional section, a writer reads a work in progress, and the members of the workshop supply direct, constructive criticism. The Featured component offers a space for more developed writers to present new works. These featured poets are members of the community who have established reputations for excellence, however, spaces are also reserved for writers who have developed sufficiently within the workshop. The Open segment gives members of the workshop a weekly opportunity to present work they have completed within the workshop. Modeled after the World Stage Jazz Workshop, a training ground for Los Angeles' top young jazz musicians, the Anasi Writer's Workshop intends to produce a cadre of writers that will equal the Watts Writers Workshop cadre of the 1960s.

Coordinating the Anasi Workshop   Michael Datcher

I learned in Poetry for the People that poetry can save people's lives. I wanted
to perpetuate that in the Black community in Los Angeles because there's such
a strong need to save lives. Part of the workshop's beauty is the range of
people who come: young brothers aged eighteen or nineteen, some in gangs,
who haven't really been politicized, Black nationalists, lesbians, and one sixty-
two-year-old woman. About fifty people in all come every Wednesday night.

Michael Datcher, a
Poetry for the People
alumnus, editor of the
highly-acclaimed
anthology of African-
American poetry, **My
Brother's Keeper**, and
the Black men's
magazine, **Image**.
(photo by Elgin Datcher)

Community-Based Poetry for the People:
Moving Poetry Beyond Academic Borders   Shelly Smith

I decided in the spring of 1994 that I wanted to start a community-based
Poetry for the People workshop in San Francisco, mostly because I always
admired the democratic spirit of Poetry for the People and felt that it should
extend beyond the boundaries of the university. So I created fliers explaining
what I hoped we could accomplish. I posted them on bulletin boards and
distributed them at open poetry readings around the city for several weeks
before our first meeting date. I was met by a diverse group of seven poets on
our first night. As we began to meet, I noticed right off the bat that
consistency and commitment were harder to come by outside of a university
setting; people showed up, and then disappeared for a couple of weeks, and
then showed up again. Most people in my particular group were interested in
just reading their poetry aloud to each other and getting criticism, rather than
discussing the possibility of doing outreach to schools, or performing. This was
a bit of a disappointment to me personally; although I think that it did create
a supportive setting for people to read their work and share inspiration. I
would offer the following advice to anyone who has never undertaken this
kind of project before (as was the case with me) :

1. Be clear on your own expectations of what you want from a group. How
   much are you willing to compromise? How much do you want to direct
   the group versus letting it go where it wants? How deep is your
   commitment? Be prepared to do a lot of calling to remind people to
   show up, of cancellations and changes, and so on.
2. If there is a community center of some kind in your area, see about
   getting a space there, rather than meeting in a café or someone's home.
   It lends an official feel to your project, provides free publicity, and may
   influence people to attend more regularly.
3. If you've never facilitated a group before or are unsure about such a role,
   consider co-facilitating with a friend.

Reading at Political Rallies   Benicio Silva

I read two poems at a big rally for Chicano students on the day when 1,500
high school students from Hayward walked out of class to protest the
substandard education they were getting. The whole walkout was organized
by a Chicano student group, and the rally itself was a chance to let students
talk to each other about what was wrong with school. I wrote what I saw in
the students' faces, the pain and anger. I wrote that there's something wrong
here—that these kids are growing up in poverty, joining gangs, dropping out.
When I got on the stage I was shaking, I was so nervous, but at the same time
it seemed as though I had been saving up my energy, anger, and frustration
for this moment. I read with anger about the unfair deportation raids on
Chicanos, about the unfair discrimination we face every day no matter what
we do or where we live. I wrote the poems for the youth because I felt their
anger and their frustration. I wanted them to know that I cared, that this
Chicano had not sold out even though he wasn't living in the barrio. And you
know what? I managed to get that energy across in my writing and my voice. I
saw them make the connections, a lot of them for the first time, between their
anger and the issues I raised.

Benicio Silva *was born in Indio, California, in 1972.*

Artwork by Poetry for
the People and
Sara Schleimer

Pass It On...   Lisa von Blanckensee

My high school lit teacher, Jamal, was in Poetry for the People in 1990-91.
When he graduated, he came to Berkeley High to teach English, which of
course for him meant teaching poetry. He taught me that I could make love to
language; he gave me a fabric scrap and a dish of sourdough starter and soon
I discovered I had a patchwork quilt, fresh bread, and friends.

When I spent spring of 1994 on independent study in Berkeley, I decided
to drop by the Poetry for the People office to see what it was all about. Pam
invited me immediately to go with the outreach committee to Highland
Elementary School to do poetry workshops with some kids there. The next
day, I had the joy of holding the hand of a fourth grade student as he slowly
wrote a poem from a painting we had brought to class. This particular student
had an overflowing imagination, but he only got a few words down because
of the time it took him to spell. By the time he finished his fourth word, the
class had begun a new exercise. He kept at it though, finding it as hard to stop
as he did to start.

I hope these kids will use their pens and confidence to secure for
themselves what they need—their gods and goddesses, their homes, the giggles
that send them shivers—and to discover what they must change. The impulses
that we have awakened in them help me in organizing a similar poetry
program at UCLA as I return this fall. I could say we are growing
exponentially, but yeasty is really a better word. It's that organic. Pass it on....

Lisa von Blanckensee *looks forward to spending more time in East Bay schools
and riding her bike when she returns from her five-year trip to Los Angeles.*

9

THROWING IT DOWN (ON PAPER, IN A BOOK)

Publishing Our Poetry

Since 1990, Poetry for the People students have self-published seven collections of multilingual, multicultural, explorative poetry. The tradition of producing these anthologies began with a leaflet of xeroxed poems stapled to a construction paper cover. The most recent edition is a full-blown, multicolored, coffee table-sized book. This last one, entitled *Poetry in a Season of Love*, presented by far the most headaches of any of them; by the time it was published, the love had gone on vacation along with all the students. From our four-plus years of mix-ups with the printer, misquoted prices, coverless anthologies, and embarrassing typos in prominent places, we present all the tips we wish someone had given us before we started.

WHY PUBLISH?

Shanti Bright

When I saw my first poem published I didn't think "Wow," but "Damn, I wrote that months ago; I've come such a long way." I guess all writers must experience regret upon seeing their work in print; a heartbreak turns frivolous very quickly, a mango metaphor turns ridiculous in minutes. But in that moment of unease, I recognized myself in an unrecognizable category: I was a writer.

Shelly Smith

Deciding whom to publish, whose words are important or good or right, whose message is valuable, is about politics. Self-publishing is about power, about taking the responsibility to disseminate your words yourself, instead of depending on being selected and approved (and edited) by a publisher who might be more interested in your marketability than your message. Those who developed feminist and Third World poetry collectives and presses in the seventies had the right idea—the economic and creative sustenance of their *own* work, and the assertion of their right to speak what they wished, as they wished, no matter what kind of threat that might pose to the powers that be. Today in San Francisco, I regularly run into musicians who are producing their work themselves, and writers who are publishing and marketing their own magazines and chapbooks. This is a radical move in a culture as market-driven as ours, not only because you're a little economic David taking on the Goliath of Corporate-Controlled Everything, but because it shows you're clear enough in the head not to believe the oh-so American hype that bigger is better, or that your worth as a writer equals your dollar worth as a writer. Now, if only people would collectivize again and invite me to join....

Trisha O'Neil

Many people in my group had written poetry privately, in their own notebooks, but few had ever read their poems out loud. For a lot of us the impact of the course came as much from sharing poetry as from writing it. People were surprised by how much they learned from the readings. But readings are only temporary. For me publishing is the ultimate, the concrete goal of the course. The anthology becomes the final committment.

Trisha O'Neil *wrote and published her first poems in Poetry for the People. She was a student athletic trainer for three years and graduated from the University of California at Berkeley in May 1993.*

FROM A STACK OF PAPER TO A BOOK: A TIMELINE

People Need to Know the Process   Sean Lewis

Like, I didn't know that there was such a thing as a bindery. That sounds so funny, but it's true. There's a funny story about the bindery. When I got the first cost quote for the book (when I told the printer what I wanted to do, with the perfect binding, and colors), a publishing house told me that the thing would cost five or six thousand dollars. I was like, "Wow, that's a lot of money. Could you itemize that for me?" And so he goes, "made out of gold," or some shit like that. So he goes through the costs for the book and he gets to the binding, and he says $800 for perfect binding. So my first quote was $800. I trusted this guy because he was a publisher, and I am a poet. He pulled that businessman-artist head trip on me.

The next place I went to, I still didn't know about the bindery. So I asked them how much they could do a bind job for. So Stan at Pill Hill Instant Printing goes, "How much were you planning on spending?" I told him that I was anticipating $800. He was like, "I could probably get it for $600 for you. I can arrange that sort of thing." So I thought: Great! I'm getting a deal. I told Bob at the Print Shop we didn't have enough money for the covers. So he said, "Let me call around for you, and we'll see if we can get a commerical rate." He calls a lot of places and they don't get back to him. But I know the places he called, right. So I called this place when I got back to June's office. And I'm like, "Is this Economy Bindery!? How much does it cost to bind 350 books?" And he asks me, "Well, who do you represent?" At this point, I catch on, so I say, "Well, I work for U.C. Berkeley." And this guy says, "Well, how does $180 sound to you?" I was like, "Hey!" So, this is divide and conquer, corporate style. That's what this is.

Sean Lewis *helped edit the anthology* Poetry for the People Presents Poetry in a Season of Love.

How To Make a Poetry Anthology Paul Manly

Buy an answering machine.
Make sure all poets know how to use the tab key on their word
processor.
Do not accept any poems with abnormal indentation.
Do not accept any poems that have five hundred one-word lines.
Tell everyone that you absolutely must have stuff one week before you
do.
Forget that
   "my cousin's
      girlfriend's
         brother-in-law
            works for a small publisher
               that works with a printer
                  that contracts with a binder
                     and he can get us a discount"
               shit.
Budget for 50% more than whatever price you're quoted.
Familiarize yourself with ratios like:
  one color per film
     three colors per proof
        300 dots per inch
           12,125 lines per page
             and 60 dollars per hour.
Start now.

Paul Manly, *Poetry for the People's computer expert/poet extraordinaire
recently graduated from the University of California at Berkeley with a degree
in Electrical Engineering and Computer Science. He is currently visiting
Zimbabwe.*

An Eight-Week Time Line: For a Full-Blown, Multi-Colored, Coffee Table-Sized Book

Eight Weeks Before Your Publication Date:
Form a committee and designate tasks. It's crucial that the committee agrees on the kind of book they want to make. The clearer you can be at this point, the less hassle you'll experience later.

Seven Weeks Before Your Publication Date:
Have all poems in hand. We set the "ironclad" deadline for submissions exactly seven weeks before we expect to finish the anthology. Of course, we find ourselves moving it back allowing for drama, trauma, and the Dalai Lama. (It's true! A couple of our cars got towed because the Dalai Lama was speaking at the Greek Theatre, so the poems didn't get turned in on time, and consequently the anthology was published four months late!)

We suggest that when you call for submissions, you let your sister and brother poets know *how* to submit their poems, so all the poems end up looking uniform in terms of type style, font size, and so on. There are basically three ways to submit a poem:

1. On computer disk
2. On paper
3. On a central computer to let each poet type in his or her own poem. This pares down formatting time.

As soon as you receive poems, start proofreading them. Twice. In *Poetry in a Time of Genocide* we messed up by miscrediting Mia Fabela-Hughes's poem, "Balloons." We'd like to take this opportunity to apologize to Mia for learning our lesson at her expense.

Six Weeks Before Your Publication Date:
Format the poems. A commercial desktop publisher will charge you about $300 to lay out only a hundred poems. Instead, we create a sense of ownership by doing the work ourselves. We used the Quark or PageMaker programs on the Macintosh, and recommend printing a 5½ x 8½ (half of 8½ x 11 paper turned sideways) book because it's the cheapest way to print.

While formatting, you'll also create the pages that come before the poetry—the title and cover pages; copyright page; any recognition you want to give your cover artist, graphic artist, editors, or printers; a table of contents; your acknowledgments; and a nice introduction. Here is a rundown:

1. Title and Cover Pages: The cover page restates the title of the book and gives a plug to the publisher. In our self-published anthologies, we call ourselves Poetry for the People Press. The title page just has the title on it.

2. Rights Page: This page is where you put your copyright year, your ISBN (International Standard Book Number), and your proper respects to the editing team, the cover and graphic artists, and your printers. To copyright your book, call the Copyright Office (202-707-3000) for an application.

3. Table of Contents: Programs such as PageMaker and Quark, and even some word processors, automatically produce a table of contents. Since the table of contents is always subject to change right to the bitter end, we've found it saves time to leave the table of contents for last.

4. Acknowledgments and Introduction: The acknowledgments section comes right after the cover page. In the introduction, we explain the concept of Poetry for the People and the theme of the anthology. Here are two sample introductions written by Carmen Thompson and Samiya Bashir.

"I trusted this guy because he was a publisher and I was a poet."
(photo by Elena Serrano)

from the Introduction to *Poetry in a Time of Genocide*

Carmen R. Thompson
November 1993

Poetry for the People: Poetry in a Time of Genocide is a title that we vigorously debated. Formally defined, genocide means, "the systematic, planned annihilation of a racial, political, or cultural group" (*American Heritage Dictionary*, 2nd Ed.). It has been a time of genocide for a long time, but each of us addressed genocide from our own particular time and space.

Is the word genocide larger than any of the interpretations we can find as a diverse group of college students? Some people argued that the word is most rightfully applied only to people living and dying in chaos in countries throughout the world. Others declared that people are living and dying in chaos right here in the United States. We never reached a consensus on this issue, but we kept the title because we think it's important that the debate be voiced.

from the Introduction to *Poetry in a Season of Love*

Samiya A. Bashir
Berkeley, 1994

By writing our poetry under the theme of *A Season of Love* we wish not to push aside or lay to rest the issues which plague our society, nor do we wish to put down our anger or exchange it for cupid's bow. What this season of love is asking us to do is to stop for a moment and remember the love that is, that must be, at the base of our anger. We are not condoning any of the ills of society, nor are we ignoring them. We are reaching inside ourselves to find the love that we have for ourselves, our world, and the people for whom we write our poetry. It is love, not hatred, that must save us, that must be at the base of any effort to save ourselves.

Five Weeks Before Your Publication Date:
Design the cover. Your anthologies will sit on shelves or in boxes if they don't really jump out at you. For this reason, the kind of cover you choose is crucial in terms of the image you want to present. It is also the most expensive part of the book. In the early days, we could only afford monochromatic covers, but recently, we got to do a full-color, glossy, elaborate, and completely professional cover, which will attract more readers.

When calling for submissions for cover art, we generally just make an announcement to the class. Word travels fast among various people's artist friends. If you need a larger pool of talent from which to choose, consider posting fliers at local art schools and cultural centers, or placing an ad in the campus or community newspaper.

After receiving submissions, we decide on a cover through a committee vote. One of the things we ask when we're voting is whether we'd consider laying down five, ten, or fifteen bucks on a book with a cover like this.

With minor work and no extra money you can assemble a back cover that rivals that of any book. The following items improve the look of the back cover and convince the faint of heart of your credible art.

1. Get praise/critical review: Write letters to established poets, professors, activists, or anyone else you can think of in your area, asking them to evaluate your manuscript and write a sentence or two to go on the back cover. Allow at least a month for responses, and include your fax number. Note: The more famous the person, the longer she or he will take to respond!

2. Definition statement: In a paragraph or so, state the objectives of the poetry collective or group, the theme of the anthology (if any), and any other details which might interest the casual bookstore browser.

3. International Standard Book Number: An ISBN is essential for distribution. To obtain one, send $165 to: ISBN Agency, R.R. Bowker, 121 Chanlon Rd., New Providence, NJ 07974, tel. 908-665-6770. You can list a price for your book in conjunction with your ISBN number, but we have always used stickers for pricing instead, since production invariably costs more than we anticipate.

4. Subject heading: On the top, right-hand corner of the back cover, you can list the subjects the anthology falls under (i.e. Poetry, Multicultural Studies, Education, Women's Studies, Gay and Lesbian Studies). This helps the bookstores place your book where it will sell.

5. Order form: We print an order form on the last page before the back cover, making ordering as easy as sticking the form in the mail.

After we have decided on a cover, we undertake the more difficult task of locating a skilled graphic artist. This person scans our art at a high resolution into a computer and shrinks or stretches it according to the dimensions of the book; leaves a half-inch for bleed and room for the thickness of the book; places our title, definition statement, critical praise, and subject heading (mindful of cost factors, spelling errors, the deadline and presentation); and calls the desktop publishing shop we're expecting to contract, asks them what kind of software they use, and formats the documents accordingly. The going rate for a graphic artist is about $25 per hour.

After getting your cover digitized, locate a printer. Five factors will determine the cost of your cover:

1. Number of colors: Covers can be printed in one color, two color, three color, or full color. More colors mean more cost, but can also make a big difference in terms of appearance.
2. Paper: Thick, good quality cover paper is a relatively cheap way to upgrade your book. The weight of the paper used for the pages will affect the "feel" of the book: heavier paper is more expensive, but light paper lets the type on the other side of the page show through.
3. Gloss: A high-quality gloss adds weight to the paper, protects the cover design from fading, and makes the book more pleasing to the eye.
4. The number of books: The unit price of the books decreases when you order more. If your budget is very tight, but you anticipate using revenues from book sales to purchase more books, consider ordering more covers than books—per copy press fees for color covers are significantly higher for short runs.
5. The printshop you use: Shop around. Ask about reduced rates for schools or nonprofit organizations. Make sure to see a sample of the printer's work—a cover that is marred with splotches or bubbles diminishes the impact of your artwork.

We spent $740 on 350 full-color, varnished, 14-point paper covers. Use this information to bargain with the printers.

To avoid simple errors that leave the publication coverless, you can invest time and money in a series of safety checks (we do):

1. Make sure to consult with all of the artists, printers, and binders you use to schedule the times that you will deliver material and the times that you need material back from them. Be sure to clarify "5 days" or "5 working days."
2. If you employ a graphic artist to work on the cover design, work closely with him or her to make sure that he or she does what you want.
3. Tell the graphic artist to leave a half-inch bleed around the edges of the cover to allow for the thickness of the manuscript—you do not want a cover smaller than your book.
4. Make sure to get the desktop publisher to run a "fiery test print" of your cover. This ensures that the graphic artist digitized your cover art correctly, and that the color separation is correct. (Once we decided to save fifty bucks and skip the fiery test run; the printer ran off three hundred covers before we realized that the person who did the separations messed up, and our colors were completely messed up. Out five hundred bucks, we couldn't release our project for another three months, and we still have the three hundred covers.)
5. Be sure to spring for a high-quality gloss for your cover. (One year, we spent money on a full-color cover on high quality paper stock, but skimped on the gloss. Even before we took the finished books out of the box, the ink began fading!)
6. Edit the back cover as carefully as you would anything else. This is the part of the book that people will look at in the bookstore and decide whether to buy your book or not. (We have neglected to edit our back cover more than once. Our "Spellbinding Poetry Anthology" turned into the "Smellbinding Hoetry Ontology" and an "exciting new series of poets," "an *exiting* new series of poets.")

Three Weeks Before Your Publication Date:
Take the disks with the digitized cover art and about 120 bucks, along with a set of instructions from your printer regarding linescreen and emulsion, to a desktop publisher. Pick up a test print of the work your graphic artist did and pay for a "color separation" of your cover.

The desktop publisher will then give you negatives of your cover (called color separations or film outputs), one for each color of your cover. (This should only take one day.) You'll then take the film outputs to a printer who specializes in covers. He or she will cast a plate using the film outputs as a model, and, reassembling the colors, essentially paint you a cover. At the same time, you'll take the manuscript to a printer who specializes in manuscripts.

Allow the printers two weeks so you don't miss your appointment at the bindery.

One Week Before Your Publication Date:
Take manuscripts and covers to a bindery for collating and binding. Using printshops that say they do both printing and binding will cost more than taking the manuscript to a bindery yourself (the printshop will take it to a bindery and charge you extra). Quality binding gives a book a flat spine, making it more visible on bookshelves than a book that is only folded and stapled.

Christine Renner,
extraordinary editor of
**Poetry for the People:
Whose Country is This,
Anyway?**
(photo by June Jordan)

from the Introduction to *Whose Country is This, Anyway*

Poetry for the People
Berkeley, 1995

"Whose Country is This, Anyway?" We are compelled to ask this question when the definition of "American" has taken on narrow and sinister connotations, and a climate of political scapegoating has given rise to such race- and class-based legislation as California's Proposition 187. Poetry for the People's basic philosophy stands against any policy that considers some people expendable. Our collective work relies on specific voices that cannot be heard unless the people who possess those voices are first respected. Poetry for the People holds to the notion that all people living in America today sustain this nation.

A Four-Week Time Line: For a Quality Anthology in a Time Crunch

We provide this section for those of you with less time to spare to produce a full-blown, multicolored, coffee-table-sized anthology. We produced Poetry for the People's Spring 1995 anthology using the following four-week time line.

Week One: Determine printing specifications for the anthology and request written bids, based on those specifications, from several printers. Consider the bids as well as reputation, professionalism, and convenience when making your final decision.

Week Two: Collect poems on disk from students and begin planning the cover design. We used PageMaker to format all of the students' poems as they would appear in the anthology.

Week Three: Give contributors a final opportunity to proofread their poems. Begin working on the introduction and acknowledgments section of the anthology. Meet with the printer to discuss the color and design of the cover.

Week Four: Complete the artwork for the cover and submit it to the printer. Approve a pre-press proof of the cover before it is printed and laminated. Do final proofreading and editing. Submit a final copy of the anthology on disk to the printer. Ask the printer for the opportunity to proof an unbound copy before final binding.

The total cost for 250 copies of our perfect bound, 5½ x 8½ inch, 164 page book with a 10 point, one color glossy cover and 60 lb paper was about $2100. When producing an anthology in a short amount of time, BE REALISTIC! You can produce a high quality book without some of the features of a more elaborate and time-consuming project.

How to Get the Money?

If you're working in a university, see if you're eligible for on-campus grants. For example, this past semester we received a publications grant from The Committee for Student Publications. The application procedures included filling out basic information and attending one or two review sessions. If you are refused funding, make sure to ask the review board why you didn't meet their requirements—they may well admire your maturity and persistence and award it to you the next time around. (It worked for us!)

If you're not affiliated with a university, you may be eligible for grants offered by local businesses, large foundations, or private donors. (We recieved an educational improvement grant from Pacific Gas and Electric for our 1991 anthology, *Poetry for the People: What Now?*) If you're affiliated with a nonprofit group and you seek money for publication or educational activities, The Foundation Center (79 Fifth Avenue, New York, NY 10003; telephone 212-620-4230 or 800-424-9836; in San Francisco: 312 Sutter Street, San Francisco, CA 94108, telephone 415-397-0902) contains a library devoted to resources for nonprofits seeking funding, as well as some resources for individual grantseekers. (Most cities have similar centers that provide grant information.) Individuals or other groups seeking grants should look at *Publication Grants for Writers and Publishers*, by Karin R. Park and Beth Luey (Oryx Press, 1991), and *Directory of Grants in the Humanities*, 8th Edition (Oryx Press, 1994).

Reminders

1. *Get everything in writing!!!* Including *anything* that a person with whom you are doing business says regarding the task they plan to perform for you. Establish a contract with each person you work with that explains what part of the publishing process they will perform and specifies agreed-upon dates, costs, and quality of work, as well as who is responsible in case of a mishap.
2. Familiarize yourself with industry standards for mess-ups. Call a printer that you're not contracting and ask how many messed-up copies per thousand they allow before you get a discount.
3. Some businesses take advantage of students and others who don't think like they do: Be prepared.
4. Proofread *everything* from cover to cover at least twice.

10

A FANTABULOUS COLLECTION
OF POEMS

The Blueprint Collective looked through four years of Poetry for the People student anthologies. We grouped the poems together according to the student anthology in which they originally appeared: *Poetry in a Time of War* (1991), *What Now?* (1991), *Power of the Word* (1992), *Poetry in a Time of Genocide* (1993), and *Poetry in a Season of Love* (1994). In the interest of democracy, and to keep the size of this collection reasonable, we reluctantly chose just one poem per poet. Unfortunately, we were unable to publish some of our favorite poems because we were not able to contact their authors for publication permission, or because we did not have the space.

The poets in this chapter range in age from eighteen to forty-four. Some have written poetry since childhood, while others wrote their first poem in Poetry for the People. They write from distinct linguistic, cultural, and historical perspectives. These poems resonate and seduce, demand revolution, and wear you out like you've danced all night. What holds this collection together is not theme, content, or technique but the poets' steady and relentless pursuit of truth.

FROM THE ANTHOLOGY
Poetry for the People In a Time of War

Untitled   Jamal Holmes

There's something you just gotta love about ya uncle
that wise old man with the top hat and white beard
          who's constantly askin for stuff
"could you go kill a couple of them colored folks for me, please
could you reach a little deeper into ya pocket for me, please
that's a nice piece of property can I have it, please?"
and he's such a sweet old man
ya just cant seem to say no
and even if ya can manage a no
he knows ya jus bein a little coy
and eventually ya mind'll change

There's something ya just gotta love about ya uncle
lookin like a thin ole St. Nick in his red and blue striped suit
when he looks into you with them eyes
and points at you with that finger
it's hard not to jus melt like butter in the sun
and when ya all soft and runny
he comes and hardens ya
with his words of wisdom
ya crawl up on his lap
and he bundles ya up in his cape
 and ya feel all warm and motivated inside
        jus ready to die   for ya uncle

"Sometimes I feel like a motherless chile,
a long way from home."

Nancy E. Johnson

On Bay Area Rapid Transit
For as long as possible.
Riding back and forth
Between the ends of the lines.
It's cold outside
For a woman with no shoes.
She sits twisting
At the red scarf on her head.
She sucks her thumb.
Looking confused
She speaks,
    "I thought I was an American."
People turn away.
    "I was born in San Francisco.
    I lived with my mother.
    I had a brother and four sisters.
    I used to go to school."
She stares at the rows of empty houses
    "I remember when there wasn't
    no B.A.R.T. train."
She looks at her hands.
Only her thumb is clean.
    "I thought I was an American
    but I'm not."
She cries and whispers,
    "I don't know where I could be from."

Poetry for the People in a Time of War

Enough Already
—4 January 1994

Claudia May

I lie on beach
cocooned by
sun rays

sand
pirouettes
beneath my fingers

A summer breeze
flickers across
the palm green sea

trees
arch backs
branches
pinch buxom fruits

birds careen
through
carmine clouds

ackees
make love
to the trees

I sip air
muscles
doze
in the lazy haze
of the sun
eyelids grow quiet
a hair of light
lulls me to sleep
and I see Jamaica
with my mother's eyes

from *This Dyke I Know*   Elizabeth Riva Meyer

"I wouldn't mind if the river took me" she says
and as our feet trace the trail
        this dirt path made to mimic the rhythm of the river
i imagine her alone
brown back drawing the sun along her course
up the river
as the rest of her body converses
with each movement and tremor
thrusting her whole self forward
she allows her body the ritual of birth
                again

and as she travels the mainstream in faith
the biology of this landscape:

        clinging algae
        granite walls
        sifted sand
        force of a torrent
guide her home

        all the elements
carrying her body in agreement

from *Aunt Ruby's House*
(part one of five)

Kelly Navies

grief
seeps thru windows
shut down too long
mingles in dust
scares away the sun
moves around the dark house
no one breathes air

no one breathes air
or listens to old songs
the 1960 stereo
crouches in the corner
condemned to silence
on the turntable
Billie Holliday
rests under the weight
of the rusty needle
waiting to sing

to sing
to Aunt Ruby
who sits alone
eyes closed to the present
held down by memories
thick as the clutter
of yellowed photographs
in her lap.

From Berkeley to Baghdad
(or Chant Down Babylon)

Matt Pigg

Underground corridor sound of sax
    Dusk and new moon
As night time neon chills
the spine
of a city/ and people
and me   not thinking
    about war
But just walking
    collar turned up
against everything uninvited
even familiar faces
With whom I'd rather not talk
    about this war
    or that rape.

So I walk my hunch-back head down shuffle
on my way to meet a friend to pass the time
    together
    five hours underground
not speaking
just   shooting   pool.

When we emerge to darkness
It must be almost morning in that land
where houses and lives burn with the sand
and sunrise brightness reveals
another beautiful day for bombing.

Mopping Up

Tomo O'Brien

Poetry for the People in a Time of War

streetsweeper beetles emerge on cue
to remove the charred residue
and sweep the fragmented remains
under the pavement

the faces with gaping holes
that neither thighskin nor concrete will repair
are scooped into the maw
and defecated into tidy piles

a quick alcohol rubdown
from tanker truck cockroaches
then squeaky clean streets greet
the trashmen of life
getting showered with tape

after the flowery speeches seep into the gutters
the cleaners arrive with dustbins
and bedpans
cart off the sundry limbs
chase off the dogs
swat the rats fat on the offal
then go home to see what they missed on TV

Tender on My Horse   Jennie Portnof

how do you taste
and you taste like this
tender on my horse or elsewhere
and according to the words the winds resume
sometimes i think i can still sense a smell of sex
all of it and its soundings inside
water turning worlds to wine
damp and hot
anger rolling off our bodies
alive and warm
you taste like arrogance

born an acolyte to bear my own blood
all of it lost for you or myself
grief and every hope i have
pulls me low towards your throat
like a drunk face to face
my breath learns the same rage riding to fly
i simply need it
i said how we've done this thing
which i like

which leaves the gates wide open
to a silent church
where i fold my hands and drink

the need to go deep
and half a world deeper

What I Mean   Leslie Shown

I mean there are better ways
to spend an evening
than yelling into the telephone
at an old lover about
how sick can a president be
to send all those young people
to the desert to die.

I mean I have better things to do
than listen to this man
who is supposed to be my friend
say that we need to stop
those barbarous Iraqi soldiers
because he read a newspaper account
of violent sexual acts
committed on small Kuwaiti girls.

I mean who do I really think might hear me
shout across three thousand miles of telephone line
that there's nothin
an Iraqi soldier might do to a Kuwaiti woman
that an American soldier wouldn't do to an Iraqi woman
that there's nothin
an Iraqi soldier might do to a Kuwaiti woman
that the Contras didn't do to a Sandinista woman
that there's nothin
an Iraqi soldier might do to a Kuwaiti woman
that an American man hasn't done to an American woman
somewhere in my neighborhood
in the last twenty-four hours.

To the Queers in Desert Storm

Vu qui Trac

The day you left
the radio blared
"I love a man in uniform"
I hear the sad song
when I look for you
in the light shows of the evening movies
rated G
where polished, hair-sprayed MC's
introduce medalled stars
who narrate
tales
without X-rated corpses showing too much flesh.
As I look for you
in the madmen's wet dreams
I never see the Hollywood casualties
the Pentagon would-be stars
Just hopeful upstarts
in the aisle waiting
to play heroes
to pay cultural dues
to die for bad art.

FROM THE ANTHOLOGY
Poetry for the People: What Now?

To the Moon   Rori Abernethy

How you doin?

Fine

You sure are

Bringin' a smile to my mind

Hey baby do you want a ride.
I know I'm on this dirt bike
but I'll take you anywhere you want
to go.
To the moon? OK
But wait a minute 'til this light
changes.

Prayer Given by and Offered to the Great Spirit

Hal BrightCloud

Hesáketvmesē, Great Spirit,

Within me and all around me,
Whose home is the immaculate void,
Within whom my body, heart, mind and soul
Find their home,

Mvtó, Thank you for your presence,
For your guidance and assistance,
For your protection,
    In this tempest of your dance.

Hesáketvmesē, Great Spirit,
Cvpóse, My grandmother.

Mvtó, Thank you for the peace
    Of the great blue sky
Mvtó, Thank you for the clarity
    Of the light of the sun
Mvtó, Thank you for the strength
    Of my Mother Earth below me
Mvtó, Thank you for the perserverance
    of life all around me.

Hesáketvmesē, Great Spirit,
Hesáketvmesē, Great Spirit,

Mvtó, Thank you for our freedom
In these, your worlds
With all their beauty and their power.

Omeka

from *Asians Don't Make Love on T.V.*   Johnson Cheu

Saw it last week
L.A. Law meets *Jungle Fever*
Jonathan and Zoe kiss slow
hot, heavy, sweat groping tongues explore
greedy for more
in bed
gettin' some.
Do you remember
the White lawyers
with lawyers, secretaries, clerks, clients
in the copy room, board room, lounge, office
even in the ceiling crawl space
in bed
gettin' some
the Black lawyers
in bed
gettin' some
Victor Sifuentes, the lone Hispanic lawyer
in bed
gettin' some
Abby and C.J.
two women kiss / the first lesbian kiss on T.V.
even Benny / the disabled clerk
got some
and still / we don't see Asian lawyers
in bed
gettin' some.
And where the Hell are the Asian lawyers anyway?
If we release our passion / it would singe the screen
    explode the picture tube
    shower glass / crack the T.V.
After all, we number a / billion in China
and growing
and we must be doing something right.

Untitled   diaab

What I like / about Wednesday
is the arch
her back makes
when she hangs her hair
down the bedside,
like a mellow note
drips from the brass / of a tenor sax
like it's got
nothing to do
but hang out.

What I like / about Wednesday
is the way
the bones in her hips
stand out
like punctuation marks,
a soft indent
to keep track / of her thighs.

Wednesday, I like
dancin all night
inches from the edge,
heat pushin in
on breath pushed out
and nothing to do
but keep the beat.

What I like
is the way she laughed
when passion broke
the bedside table.
A splash of wine
and the afterglow,
Ah, I
do like Wednesday.

Conjugations (While Teaching English)   Cindy Franklin

We conjugate *to be*
in the chill church air
knees to chests in too-small chairs
I am fever: Fabio Serrano
craves *pupusas*, peanut butter
the touch of the son
he has never seen
though he felt his kick
his hard pregnant presence
Esteban Marino de Paz, his child, now 5,
is still alive
while his shot-dead friend Fabio lies in some field
    he had to fly, time only
      to take the name Fabio
      and leave his own (Esteban) behind
in the green of El Salvador

Stories like these come into the room
uninvited. They arrive
with a word as simple as *sister*,
slip in with *cousin, brother, mother, wife*
Even *to be* is risky   irregular
So many still open absences to be
tongued over
Today we stay with safe words
    like *aspirin, apricots asbestos*
We make a tree of the future
tense *to be*

After class
Fabio will sit straightbacked at the table
his silver rings will move
with the brown of his hands
orchestrating
    food banks

clothing drives
employment and shelter for his people
for his people
outside the church they are planting a garden
the upturned soil, shot with green
beginnings for what is
to be

love poem for george bush   Shelly Smith

you don't even remember
you liked to touch yourself tender & slow
maybe your momma screamed
threatened to cut it off

you don't even remember
violet twelve-year-old thirst for another child's flesh
scented like sweat & peanut butter & summer
you don't even remember that young fast impulse to give
someone a slice of yourself sweet & huge
you don't remember cuz you don't know
hot or soft/you don't know
safe or warm

and you never rocked with another/never cried together
like baby panthers to the stars
and you never felt longing like cream on the tongue
and you never lay down to love like thunder
electric & wet/you never lay down
you never lay down/you never lie down

cuz you think lie down you think defeat. die. weak.
so you'll never regret Hiroshima/ Nagasaki/Vietnam/ Iraq
you'll never regret frying children with your precious white light
you'll never regret tossing Haitians to the sea
you'll never regret/people dying of AIDS
people dying of empty stomach/people dying of government

you're too bitter
toward mother for screaming/sealing the soft place
toward Navy for teaching your soul to march & talk death talk
toward enemy/always enemy/always elsewhere/always
monster/always other

and if it ain't Russia well it's Iraq
it's the dark & savage nations who can't govern themselves for shit
or if it's here at home well it's darker people/poorer people

who can't take care of themselves for shit
it's homosexuals just asking for diseases
it's goddamn whining females
it's the idiot boy who scuffed your shoes/last time he shined 'em

and if it's closer still well it's your wife who stole your freedom
it's your mistress who ruined your marriage
it's your mother who killed the soft place
it's your father who abused you
with indifference and cash

you can't imagine an enemy closer still/than your wife
than your mother/than your father
you can't imagine an enemy who lives where the soft place was
who lives for father in absentia/who lives in your hollow heart
your regimated soul/your long lost capacity to love

You are the other
you are the killer
you are the savage
you are the pervert
and you'll never lie down/and you'll never warm up
and you'll never find peace
and you'll never make love/you'll never make love
you'll never make love

and when you go down small and mean as your life
I won't cry for you/can't feel sorrow for no loss at all

instead
I'll tiptoe to a place/soft & indigo
I'll meet my love there with a slice of myself
warm & huge
and we'll cry like panthers
we'll succumb to the waves
we'll succumb to the thunder
in our lying down
together
we'll succumb

FROM THE ANTHOLOGY
Poetry for the People: The Power of the Word

This Sister I Know   Michael Datcher

Raised in the hood
And raced out
Fast as
The bus
Escaping to
The white school
The first
Black Cheerleader
Leading
The white boys
Cheers
For the brothers
On the court
Who magically became
Niggers
In the class
Just like her

*"Without fear of being happy"**   Mateo Roose

Revolution is not
        gun-toting, tough-talking men
   or mighty and militant sloganeering

Revolution is not based on
        bombs, rocks, bullets, and battles
   or any "prolonged peoples' insurrection"

Revolution is
   the persevering smile
       a daring laugh
           uncompromising joy

the refusal to let humanity slip out of humans' hands

   In revolution
       a teardrop is not surrender
          it is confrontation

       and love is not weakness
       but a guarantee for victory.

*electoral slogan of Brazilian Worker's Party in 1989 elections.

FROM THE ANTHOLOGY
Poetry for the People: Poetry in a Time of Genocide

from *42 Percent of All Indian Women of Child-Bearing Age in 1974 Had Been Involuntarily Sterilized*   Shanti Bright

Just some doctor
Not the BIA like in '74
who thought hysterectomy meant his choice

Ripping into her
Digging out her
Leaving her
vacant and empty
She cannot dance.

If he were impotent
would he beg me
to cut off his dick?

Doctors say old
I see sweaty running
in ripe green hills. Wild
and laughing like coyote
he cages.

In dreams I see her
shrunken and wrinkled
concave stomach like sallow land
not ripe mango I yearn.

She cannot bear more survivors
but her stories of Oklahoma
lush and sweaty
remind me of her
womb, safety I want
to crawl into.

from *Ah-ma Ti*   Jane Chen

each imitated forced syllable
draws her
daughters granddaughters
closer to the american shore

closer   so her only living son-now-ucla-doctor can display her—
         "uneducated peasant mother"— to jocular colleagues
closer   so the white bagboy at safeway can glare in her direction
         as she fumbles
         to distinguish coin values by faces
         jeffersonlincolnwashington
         howcanyoutellthemapart?   theyalllookthesame
closer   so my brother and i could
         stare   shamestruck
         as she tripped over english

         we shed the verbal birthmarks of yellow
         inferiority that year in Mrs. Adams's class

1992
Ah-ma wakes
wordlesss at gray yellow dawn
her daily lone walk awaits i lie beside her
breathing   quiet   in awe of
the woman
who first taught me to love women
                                to speak

despite all
threats of annihilation

Untitled

Aboji, you say to me, "Miguk un cho ji an na"
And that I can never be American
Because the blood in me is Korean
All my life you stressed only the importance of speaking,
mastering English
While in school teachers beat the language / the Korean out of me
I learned real fast
how keeping your mouth shut / can get you far in America
Teachers adored me
I wanted to scream, to cry / to explode
And let those ignorant teachers know / I had much to say
    but lacked the words to say it
For many years, I thought / speaking Korean was wrong
And to be Korean was shameful
So you see
I lost my tongue, my voice, my meaning
    long ago
In America, colored immigrants are de-humanized and
culturally bastardized
And if you're not white, you're never quite

Now I hear
I gotta serve as some sort of model minority
White America thinks Mexicans and Blacks
Should imitate my silence, obedience, and confusion
No fucking way

So father / rest assured
you're right
America's not so great
But also face,
that the price you paid
    by bringing me here is that I'll never know
        what it means
          to be
            Korean

A MAN!

Seyyida Saterfield

I met a man
Did you hear what I said?
A MAN

Not a pimp / Not a player / Not a cheater
Not a "mac-daddy" / Not a woman beater
Not a liar / Not a fool / Not a jerk
Not an irresponsible ass hole / Not an insensitive bastard
Not a "jack me off, baby please, baby please" sex fiend
    who ain't gettin' none
But A MAN

I ain't gotta hear no B.S. 'bout
"I can't come over tonight, I got hella shit to do
and I sho can't take you out 'cause I ain't got no money"
Which clearly explains why they look like Neiman Marcus on wheels
And don't do nothin 'cept drink 40's, play dominoes and spades

But I ain't worried
'Cause Ima let boys be boys
Play with themselves, toy guns and balls
On cement play grounds
And one day they'll hit their heads against the concrete
Wake up / Want women
But, only see little girls playin' the same games

Yep, I found a man
His hands rays of sun
Caress my glistening skin
As I walk on hot West Indian sands

This brotha
Don't make my stomach turn
Or hot lava drops drip from eyes

He put goose bumps down my spine
I smile
'cause Bob wail "No Woman No Cry"

FROM THE ANTHOLOGY
Poetry for the People: Poetry in a Season of Love

Giant Steps   Renata Archie

i couldnt even hum it
but coltrane
tol me
his
favorite things
so im gonna tell
you how
        when you the sun
set peach purple
and a rainbows on the right
whisperin to us bout
lush damp green
brown everywhere
        i arch
to kiss
your horizon where
we make mahogany
silver cloud streaks

but i couldnt do that before

Mother Magic

Alegria Barclay

Mother makes me Easter baskets
rings the doorbell
and leaves them on the step
for me to find
my intelligence insulted at seven.
I claim the bunny's nonexistence
but still she bothers to make me believe,
says fantasy needs more friends.
And on Chinese New Year's
gives me little red envelopes
full of money, magic, candy, crayons
her care.
The house smells of simmering,
kitchen sweat and lemon grass.
I dream of dumplings,
spring rolls spread across the table,
some pork chops to put America on the menu
for my dad.

And in this place
I come home to / frightened and fretful
'cuz a boy said / "a black man can't marry a white woman"
thinking maybe I was illegal,
mother massages my mind
tells me love is liquid
you're an ocean if you're open.

Painting with watercolor,
roses, pieces of thread
on the porch covered / with the pictures of lovers
my mother whispers these words:
"You're a mixed medium masterpiece.
When you combine earth and sky / you get a world
you're a world of wonder,"
and smells my dark skin deep:
a Vietnamese kiss.

from *Untitled*

Cruz Joel Angeles

1

Marcha!
en la calle Broadway / in L.A.
unos ocho mil
cargando vanderas a frente
Dile "NO!" al 187
todos latinos presentes
defendiendo los derechos de mi gente
no somos comunistas
ni siquiera contrabandistas
solo imigrantes
con esperanzas brillantes
gritando y cantando / "Sacaremos ese buey de Sacramento!"
por su intento / de chingar al imigrante
él que sostiene
con todo sudor en la frente
la vida de este continente.

2

Pero el gringo Wilson
nos culpa a nosotros por la recesión
nos quiere hecha a la migración
pa' ganar la elección.
por eso es que la gente protesta
marchando hasta el city hall
porque si el Wilson
ganas las elecciones
no podremos mandar a nuestros hijos
a la escuela para darle sus educaciones
invitaciones / a la vida buena
con comida caliente en la mesa
ropa lujosa y toda la cosa
el sueño de ser alguien con éxito
sin ser discriminado, maltratado
o ser llamado "mojado!"

sesame street never meant that much to me   Marcos Ramirez

johnny/ tonito/ mis hermanos
i remember/ shimmy-shimmy Coco Pop
shimmy-shimmy shy
freeze tag/ cartoon tag/ Gringo tag/ n mud pies
hide n seek/ kickball/ stickball/ n Applejax
poprocks/ lollypops / purple drippin missile pops
scooby doo on da tube / askin where are you/ n we say
trick or treat smell my feet
give us anything to eat
tell us how to get to sesame street
so we can play every day of the week
so no one call us dirty Mexicans
cuz we use our "Spanish lexicon"
n no one make fun of our clothes
cuz we deep/ down/ Richmond po
n i remember
ping pong/ Donkey Kong / n delicious Ding Dongs
Sidewalk Sundaes/ Super Slushees
n strawberry Kool-Aid
Coca-Cola/ Cracker Jacks / two pieces of a Kit Kat
hop scotch/ double dutch / momma's famous christmas punch
those damn kids from da brady bunch
showin us what we ain't got
n how in hell could we have forgot
po people minds/ sharp/ slickity-zip/ n quick
fuck sesame street
n the brady kids too
cuz they never talking bout / what we remember
n what we seen
fuck da prom
n them stupid puppets too
we wanna know / how to get
how to get the fuck outta
poverty street
without bein jan brady white

Caged

Stephanie A. Rose

inside these bars
i don't remember what laughter / feels like
i sit vigil for / each beat of my heart
growl of my stomach / throb of my head
i can only see my body
in the darkness of my cage

i try to break out of my skin
but that only brings blood
and i taste it all the time anyway

so i swallow a pill and
the clouds break away and
it seems like the first time
i've ever seen the sun

my high disappears sudden as
lightening streaks a calm sky
my damp cell reeks of self hatred
as i succumb to shadows that
bring curdled milk and green apple sauce

outside these bars you
preach that "normal" has no meaning
but if you wore my cement shoes and / then tried to fly
you'd see my vision thick
as your chemically-balanced head

i feel the hairs on my legs / trying to escape my body
and i want to follow

drums pound my temples
pushing life through / my pores
and i grope for it

can i blame / misaligned stars
and fluctuating hormones
or should i question my sanity again?

poem for the young white man who asked lorna dee
how she, an intelligent, well-read person
could believe in the war between races   Shelly Teves

(inspired by lorna dee cervantes and dedicated to cesar arce)

> you may not believe
> in the war between races
> right now / cuz masters
> the man that gunned down
> one chicano tagger
> and injured another
> ain't aimin his at you
> misteryoungwhiteman
> who sits suited in a cushy chair
> and tsk tsk tsk / shaking your head at the sunday
> propaganda / passed off as news
> you use hype / to hide the truth
> from yourself
>
> so you sound sincere / when you say—Look, see
> it's all right here in the San Francisco Chronicle and I quote
>
> *William Masters says he was just out for a late night*
> *stroll around his neighborhood two weeks ago. As usual,*
> *he carried his unlicensed handgun in his fanny pack.*
> *By the next morning, a teenage Latino grafitti vandal*
> *was dead and another was shot in the rear...*
>
> end quote, so there.
>
> when you finish
> reading your front page sedation
> you feel sleepy in your world
> where the brown boys you call
> vandals are not people
> and no one really fired

the semi-automatic / wounding david hillo
and killing cesar arce / a young man
with a name and a family
but you read him only as enemy
so you applaud william masters
the former marine
trained to take out as many as he could
when he calls arce a mexican skinhead
you nod yours and say—Good, somebody's got to do something
because crime
in California's gotten way out of control.

well don't tell me about it
misteryoungwhiteman
cuz i know / the criminals have free reign
in this land / where masters receives praise
from newspapers and talk radio
where well-wishers tie up his phone all day
where the l.a. county d.a. declares
the shooting of david hillo
and the killing of cesar arce
a "justifiable act of self-defense"
even though masters buried those bullets
in the brown skin on their backs
where your war on crime is
a war on my sisters and brothers
and your crime bill is
a declaration of that war
where you can sit suited / glossed-over and confused
cuz you hid the truth so good from yourself
you thought you could fool everyone else

well you may not believe
in the war between races
right now / pal
but you better watch
your back

Becoming Again

Pamela Wilson

I missed the screams
the fighting and surrender
but saw the long-wounded
expiring on the field.

The ghosts
alive and dead
drifted away
with glazed eyes / gone quiet.
Shock quiet.

God.
The field.

Walking downhill
I knelt beside a stream of blood / sticky and black
and I licked up the gore
swallowing
even the fragments / of bone.

Then straightened and screamed
till the carrion birds took wing
and I saw quills begin to sprout
from the follicles on my arms.

I became
that day
god
the gods
and the people.

Now I slit my wrists
where ever I go
and let children lick me
as long as they like.

11

CODA

I ain't goin nowhere unless you come with me
I say I ain't goin nowhere lessen you come with me
I ain't about to be some leaf that lose its tree
So take my hand see how I'm reachin out for you
Hey here's my hand see now I'm reachin out for you
We got a whole lot more than only one of us can do

—June Jordan

Travelin' Shoes (for June Jordan)   Ruth Forman

June,
    I remember your blues words, pieces of a blues collective, from our first
poetry reading.
    The one that came from us around the table in 102 Barrows with our
poetry guidelines and you sitting at the end challenging us but with laughter,
always with laughter. Was it 102 Barrows? Whatever room it was, in the
middle of all that theory and ivory tower, we noticed something real going on.
Something magical. We say sometime soon we're all going to look back at
these days how you and Alice Walker, Barbara Christian, and Toni Morrison do
at that big photograph on Barbara's wall.

In Barrows and Dwinelle and in that room at the top of all them damn steps, we knew something wonderful going on. The class grew larger to Poetry for the People, Vietnamese and Chicano, Israeli and Angelino, Blackfoot and African, wheelchair user, womanist, feminist, gay, straight, of Color, American, defined as we pleased. We all knew something special going on. Because somewhere behind the hip glasses and fresh cut, somewhere deep behind the teeth you say, like on that blues night, you want us to come with you.

June, you are far from a leaf. You are far from a leaf but the deep colors of sunrise and sunset. The same that bring the old words and whispers and somehow we remember everything, all that we come from and where we go. We find age in ourself and trunk at our back, root at our feet, buds in our fingertips. Lady, you are more than a leaf, even the prettiest one we fight over to keep between our pages. You between root and branch, soil and sky: we see you challenge tangling words that hover our eyes, prevent any people from entering our head, clutter our minds, dry up our tongues and make us thirsty for something real and living. Worthy to be touched.

Such example. In your work you name specifics we cannot deny. Broken coffee tables, legs, fingers, rocks against stone, pieces of children and pieces of sand. Soweto to Palestine, South Central to Baghdad. You bring us home and fathers and family and mothers, laundry and children. And the peace with which you name the wars. Regular as breakfast, calm as afternoon. How the twenty-first century must rejoice you, you who remind us that suffering, no matter what language, is suffering and love, no matter what place, is love. And you move us beyond the cold places. You validate first instincts before they are reshaped into the numbness of a greater unconsciousness. Your words ring familiar, and then the world is no longer so complicated. Blood is blood, bone is bone, steel is steel. You call it how you see it.

Maybe that is how you can laugh. And how your laugh is so full and clear. Maybe that is how you walk head above the sidewalk, because you can embrace this world with intimacy. Maybe numbness is what makes so many of our heads heavy and looking at the cracks. Not to say that I don't wonder if the world is heavy to you some mornings. I know it is. But somehow maybe to see it and live in it full and clear it is all right.

In that room in Barrows, you brought me to that place. Challenged my fingers to touch that tree you won't lose, find the heavy grooves of my people, the beauty in resistance and language of Langston Hughes, Angela Grimke, Phillis Wheatley, and countless others. I know they are part of the roots with no beginning and no end. I know I am part of the roots with no beginning and no end. The ones that whisper real things up to the leaves that tell the river that tell the sky that rain back to the soil and make the rocks solid. You offer us center and within it our truth.

You bring me find it. In the sidewalk and loose change, double-dutch and sunset, mango and sweet sweat, afro pick, jheri curl, kitchen naps, Detroit, and sky-blue Cadillacs. You bring us find it, crows and rice, missiles and zoot suits, figs and olive trees quivering beneath the tongue naked in our particular shade of language. You bring us find it out gold and necessary. I saw you do it. You bring us find it somewhere between clearing throat and hot cheek. You bring us find our language rooted in both directions and in it we find strong thighs and bare ankles and it is all right.

It is all right to jive intimately with the world. To intimately know those experiences around us, to call it out without fear because where we see from and speak from is a valued place. You teach us this place as truthful and unshakable and we speak from there. Trembling voices and goose bumps but determination and raw power.

We have power in learning what we have to say is not only valid but necessary. Homegirl we celebrate it because it is so nice to be important and in good company. It is so nice to sweat for something that they will never take away. Homegirl we celebrate because there is so little left to celebrate ourselves sometimes and with these roots we know we have something. And we celebrate cause we can name our enemies name our fears without the knees shaking anymore name those homeless words to a place they belong no longer around our necks. You push us to locate our voices despite a language that teaches us distance from our own homes. And we can celebrate each other in this process for now our words know exactly their meaning, their place in the context of this world, and we are a different people and we are not alone.

So this is to say, June, that we watch you usher in the next century. Your students from Barrows and Dwinelle and that big room at the top of all them damn steps. You teach us call it as it is for those experiences important to us, but also to go beyond community, go beyond country, go beyond this world to ourselves in relation to it and not this world in relation to us. This is where we go. Aware and learning to be unafraid. Thank you for this vision to name it as we see it in our particular shade of language and experience, offering hopefully, as bell hooks challenges (from a speech given at Women's Voices, Los Angeles Festival in September 1993), "voices that move beyond pain to offer the remembrance of hope." That is what gives God's children travelin' shoes. You between where we've come from and what we have to do. Thank you for the shoes. Yes, there is so much more than only one of us can do and we come with you.

How This Blueprint Was Written...   Lauren Muller

in one month with lots of pizza, lentil soup, apples, jasmine tea, toast, tostada chips, and occasionally, some chocolate.... Four poets wrote quietly and intently in the bedroom; in the study and in the kitchen, there were five computers, and facing each screen were two or three poets negotiating word choice, examples to prove a point, and paragraph placement.

On the stairs an intense discussion took place between two women: "Okay, I understand how it felt to write that poem, but how did it feel when you read it aloud? When you went public with it? Have you shown it to your mother?"

Serious discussion buzzed everywhere.

"Why is it important to publish your poetry?"

"How do the workshops work?"

"What's the connection between your poem and some unknown person who might want to read it?"

Meanwhile, the phone kept ringing with calls from New York and Boston and Ireland and Berkeley, and tremendous excitement was everywhere as reunions took place and Poetry for the People alumni met with new comrades.

From downstairs, my neighbors called to complain about the noise. "What's going on?"

Well, we were writing a book!

None of this process was easy. Every single sentence went through several hands; this was truly a collaboration if, in fact, ever there were such a thing!

In our first draft, we used the word "you" to address the reader, but then we realized it sounded too didactic. So we decided to use the word "we" and talk about ourselves. Finally, we realized a necessity to use the word "I" and to bring in personal testimonies of all sorts.

At the beginning, I don't think anyone could have used the first person pronoun, but the hard work of composing this Blueprint led us to that place of confidence and clarity.

Between computer breakdowns, and relationship breakups, and people looking for jobs and somewhere to live, this Blueprint came to life, straightforward and from the heart.

September 15, 1994

Creating a Poetry for
the People Blueprint!
Gary Chandler, Lauren
Muller, Elizabeth Meyer,
and Stephanie Rose
conspire and
collaborate.
(photo by Shanti Bright)

Ruth Forman with June
Jordan. Ruth is the
winner of the 1992
Barnard Women's
Poetry Prize for her
book **We Are the Young
Magicians**. She is a
Poetry for the People
alumnus and friend.
(photo by Jamal Holmes)

Creating a Poetry for
the People Blueprint!
Elizabeth Meyer and
Shanti Bright take a
break in front of the
guaranteed-to-crash
computers.
(photo by Lauren Muller)

INDEX OF COAUTHORS AND CONTRIBUTORS